CAMBRIDGE LIBRARY COLLECTION

Books of enduring scholarly value

Music

The systematic academic study of music gave rise to works of description, analysis and criticism, by composers and performers, philosophers and anthropologists, historians and teachers, and by a new kind of scholar - the musicologist. This series makes available a range of significant works encompassing all aspects of the developing discipline.

Music and Education

Published in 1848, this short work by Joseph Mainzer (1801–51) argues for the considerable value of music as part of general education. A German priest, teacher and composer, Mainzer had an important influence on the development of amateur music and the choral movement in the first half of the nineteenth century. Attracting large numbers of adult labourers, he gave free singing classes, using his own highly influential teaching system. Music, Mainzer argues here, not only brings direct moral and social benefits, but also takes the place of potentially harmful habits and leisure activities, such as the drinking of alcohol. The work defines music in relation to its educational value and potential, exploring the origins, development and moral influence of music since the ancient Greeks. Mainzer also discusses the ways in which music is taught at all levels.

Cambridge University Press has long been a pioneer in the reissuing of out-of-print titles from its own backlist, producing digital reprints of books that are still sought after by scholars and students but could not be reprinted economically using traditional technology. The Cambridge Library Collection extends this activity to a wider range of books which are still of importance to researchers and professionals, either for the source material they contain, or as landmarks in the history of their academic discipline.

Drawing from the world-renowned collections in the Cambridge University Library and other partner libraries, and guided by the advice of experts in each subject area, Cambridge University Press is using state-of-the-art scanning machines in its own Printing House to capture the content of each book selected for inclusion. The files are processed to give a consistently clear, crisp image, and the books finished to the high quality standard for which the Press is recognised around the world. The latest print-on-demand technology ensures that the books will remain available indefinitely, and that orders for single or multiple copies can quickly be supplied.

The Cambridge Library Collection brings back to life books of enduring scholarly value (including out-of-copyright works originally issued by other publishers) across a wide range of disciplines in the humanities and social sciences and in science and technology.

Music and Education

JOSEPH MAINZER

CAMBRIDGE
UNIVERSITY PRESS

CAMBRIDGE
UNIVERSITY PRESS

University Printing House, Cambridge, CB2 8BS, United Kingdom

Published in the United States of America by Cambridge University Press, New York

Cambridge University Press is part of the University of Cambridge.
It furthers the University's mission by disseminating knowledge in the pursuit of
education, learning and research at the highest international levels of excellence.

www.cambridge.org
Information on this title: www.cambridge.org/9781108064774

© in this compilation Cambridge University Press 2013

This edition first published 1848
This digitally printed version 2013

ISBN 978-1-108-06477-4 Paperback

MUSIC

AND

EDUCATION.

BY

Dr. MAINZER.

LONDON:

LONGMAN, BROWN, GREEN, AND LONGMANS,
PATERNOSTER-ROW.

EDINBURGH: ADAM & CHARLES BLACK.

MDCCCXLVIII.

DEDICATED

MEMBERS OF THE

EDUCATIONAL INSTITUTE OF SCOTLAND.

CONTENTS.

INTRODUCTORY REMARKS.

At the conclusion of the Annual Report of the High
School of Edinburgh, (1847,) we read the following
lines by Dr. Schmitz, its Rector :—

"In regard to singing, no one in our days will
venture to deny the salutary, refining, and moral influence which the practice of the art of music in general, and especially the music of the human voice, exercises upon youthful minds ; and it is confidently
hoped, that both the patrons of the High School and
the public at large, will heartily welcome and sanc-
tion the introduction of so powerful an agent, in inspiring our youthful pupils with a love of what is noble
and beautiful. Singing once was the glory of Scotland ; and may it again become an ornament to the
country, and serve in our churches to enhance our best
feelings of piety and devotion."

This question of the introduction of singing into the High School came before the Town Council on the 21st September. Bailie Duncan, who had, with some others, been appointed as member of a committee to examine this subject, made his report, advising :[1] *that singing should not be taught; that the Scottish mind was not prepared for it; and that he could not see what connection Music had with Greek.* (A laugh.) At the same time that the Town Council of Edinburgh was carrying such resolutions, committees were forming in several towns of Scotland for the promotion of musical instruction in schools and classical institutions ; and from some of these towns we received letters, in which the writers, as by common consent, protested against the opinion of the City Magistrates in regard to the ripeness of Scotland for music. A teacher of the Canongate passed a more severe sentence on this decision, in saying, that he hoped the Town Council had only meant Edinburgh, and not the Canongate, as there the mind was quite prepared, and singing had been taught a long time. We fear, when we examine the question more closely, that it is not the Scottish mind, but the mind of the Town Council of Edinburgh, that is unprepared.

Since the Town-Council is not yet prepared to make mathematics, history, and the physical sciences, indispensable branches of a curriculum in a High School, can we expect it should be more so for the

---

[1] See *Scotsman* of 22d September 1847.

cultivation of the fine arts ?   Let us suppose that Latin and Greek had never been taught, and that their
introduction had been proposed instead of music; we
should have read in the *Scotsman* of the 22d, that the
College Bailie had moved, and that the Council had
unanimously approved of the resolution, that Greek
and Latin should not be taught; that the Scottish
mind was not prepared for it; and that they could not
see what connection these dead languages, the tongues
of heathen philosophers and popish priests, had to do
with the present youth of Scotland, who had a great,
and very pardonable predilection for the language of
their ancestors, and were not at all inclined to ex-
change it ! (Sensation.)

   Although much inclined to indulge in a further
analysis of the exposition which the Town-Council
have made of their sentiments in regard to music, yet
we abstain.   We remark only, that we intended to
address a letter to the Lord Provost, Bailies, and
Councillors, on their resolution of the 21st September,
but the letter became a book.   Should they find it
surprising that they occupy a place in it, may they
consider, that since they have spoken of music, music
has a right to speak of them.   They will understand
in what relation music stands to the Town-Council,
although they cannot see what connection it has with
Greek.

   At all events, the friends of youth, the friends of
education, those who appreciate music as an educational element, will thank me for having raised this

little public monument in honour of the Magistrates, as a memento of their services and patronage, bestowed with such lustre and enlightened views, upon science, literature, and art, especially that art which has been treated by them with such peculiar favour, and has enjoyed their unanimous recommendation, that it should not be taught: words of oracular importance, and which will mark a glorious epoch, both in the history of music and that of Town-Councils in Scotland.

PREFACE.

Dr. Johnson said, in his *Journey to the Western Islands:* "The character of a schoolmaster is less honourable in Scotland than in England; it is therefore seldom accepted by men who can adorn it." Scotland seems to have but little felt this stigma thrown on the profession of the teacher, and the want of appreciation of so important a ministry of the public welfare. Almost a century passed, and not a step was taken towards its intellectual and social advancement. The teacher at last, filled with the importance of his mission, and forced by the claims which the progress of time and civilization imposed on him, rose to efface, from his profession and his country, a reproach unworthy of both. He thus called to his brethren : Let us advance in knowledge ! let us study ! let us unite ! if union be strength, study is knowledge !

The call was heard and re-echoed from every hill and every shore ; the light of hope, like the beacon-fire of former days, was seen from every village, and in a moment there stood eighteen hundred teachers, as

a phalanx united, ready to defend the rights and claims
due to the youth, and to the honour of their country.
The National Schools in Ireland, the Teachers
Union of England, and the Educational Institute of
Scotland, are heralds of a new era in the history
of education in Great Britain. The hour in which
the latter was decided, we consider the hour of the
emancipation of the teacher in Scotland. From being
the neglected, the despised member of society, he will,
by his talents, superior accomplishments, and public
usefulness, rise and reach that station which he deserves,—he in whose hands are the morality and
happiness of the coming generation. This Institute,
which placed itself high above all sectarian differences, and has thus shewn a superior spirit quite in
conformity with the age, and worthy of the high vocation of the teacher, will become a powerful lever to
raise the social and intellectual standing of that profession which cannot but be considered as one of the
mightiest pillars of society and nations.

In dedicating the present work to the Educational
Institute of Scotland, we do so, not that we deem
the teachers particularly learned in music, or that they
have bestowed particular attention on it, either as a
science or an art; but because the Institute has, de-
spite the national prejudices, acknowledged music as
a branch of public instruction, as an element in the
education of youth.

Yet there are still some who would rather impede
than favour its cultivation in schools, as much from

a disappreciation of it, as from an exaggerated importance of the branches they teach. It can be demonstrated, that hitherto the Scottish teachers and the Scottish clergymen are infinitely behind the rest of Europe in the knowledge of music. The stern Covenanter, though he fought at the battle of Drumclog and Bothwell Bridge, to the tune of *John come kiss me now*, or died singing psalms in the midst of the crowd at the Grassmarket, or on the heather of his solitary moors ; yet, his fright of a fiddle, or a dance, in which he always saw the cloven foot behind, has become well nigh the general feeling of Scotland with regard to music. On the other hand, singing has been too much associated with drinking ; many sing only when they are drunk. Can we wonder, then, that Music is not considered an agent of mental and moral culture by those who know it only as an art of debauchery, the priestess of revels and public-houses ? Can we be surprised that young men are peculiarly guarded against music, when it is considered to be to them, what the flame is to the moth—destruction ? But even this fear is a new homage of its power, a genuflection before its throne. The young man who knows music is sought, is courted, and carried along in the whirlpool of youth. If he were the rule and not the exception, were there many such musical phœnixes, the individual would not be so much thought of. If the family afforded recreation through music, they would not want to seek it elsewhere. A country which has allowed the

art to sink to so low an ebb, wears, like the galley-
slave, the chain of its own guilt. How couldst thou
forget, land of song, home of the bard, "meet nurse
of a poetic child," Caledonia! that there is also a
holy music, a music that lives, and loves, and suffers
with us, that raises the soul, bent in sorrow, out of the
dust, and bears it beyond the clouds; a music that,
like an aurora of eternity, penetrates into the night
of life, cheers and illumines our path! how couldst
thou forget that, like the rainbow, music is a me-
morial of a covenant between the earthly and the
celestial, blending equally, and reflecting all colours!
that she has accents for all nations, all ages; that
every epoch of our life has its own tones: that to
the boy she appears, with his spring, his plays, his
birds and butterflies; to the adolescent with his love
for every thing that is beautiful, great and elevating,
for liberty and country; to the aged a sweet ripe
fruit of life and wisdom, a setting sun that throws a
purple veil over days and recollections of the past, and
brightens the pilgrim's path towards futurity. He
who thus penetrates and reveres music, to him she is
the virgin of charity, who, with her love, her tears,
and her inspiring breath, is near him in all moments
and trials of life, a sister-soul in whose bosom he con-
fides every silent thought, and every emotion.

Thus has the Scottish Institute looked upon music,
and therefore has it acknowledged it an educational
element; a late and feeble homage paid to the art, but
a distant foreboding of better days to come. As it ap-

pears to us as a pharos of hope in the darkness of the
night, we have associated our thought and our work
with theirs ; and in exposing our principles, hope to
strengthen and support their own, and shew how, in
united zeal and activity, they can be realized for a
country's welfare, and a nation's glory.

Music will no longer be a destitute child of perse-
cution : it will become a welcome guest under every
roof, in every cottage. Soon the youth will cease to
be mute ; not a hundred children, but a hundred
schools, will unite in love, and harmony, and inno-
cence. In those sublime moments, when simple but
graceful strains are carried upon thousands of infant voices, all will feel the power of the multitude,
as Haydn did, in tears, when he heard the charity
children of St. Paul's ; or, overcome by the majesty
of simple grandeur, exclaim with Catalani, when she
heard the primitive chants of the Grecian Church :
" My song is of this world, but this is a choir of
angels."

MUSIC AND EDUCATION.

~~~~~~~~~~~~~~~~~

I.

MUSIC originates daily among us, as it originated thousands of years ago, under all climes, among all nations of the earth; for nature follows unchangeable laws. Sound, the first element of music, ere it rises to that degree of charm and power by which our admiration is fixed, presents itself as a very simple physical phenomenon, as the result of vibration communicated by the air. In this, its elemental state, it not only strikes our ear and acts on our nerves, but exercises an influence, more or less sensible, on objects even of inanimate creation. If we proceed from this point, and if we advance from the simple sound, the breath of air, towards the immensity of the ideal world in which it reigns as art, a whole empire lies extended before us, in which the soul feels as in a land of wonder and enchantment.

Every tightened string which vibrates in the air, every hollow tube through which the wind passes, taught man the use of instruments. A thick or long string or tube produces deep sounds; a thin or short, high ones. In this simple discovery lies the principle of all stringed and wind instruments. If the string be stretched upon a piece of wood, the finger which presses upon the board diminishes its length,

A

and, consequently, raises the sound. The same result is obtained by making holes in the iron tube, or the wooden pipe. By covering or uncovering these holes with the fingers, we render the column of air contained in the tube longer or shorter, which, set in motion by the wind, or by the mouth, gives higher or lower notes. The notes which chance seems at first to produce, are, by a little skill and observation, brought into connection, and thus the regular scale of ascending and descending notes is established. When once in possession of an instrument, giving a more or less limited series of sounds, we begin to employ these sounds in a successive or inverted order, and thus produce a tune or melody. We select the notes from the scale, and compose a musical idea, as words and thoughts are expressed, by bringing the letters of the alphabet into a certain connection with each other. Thus music has been taught us by nature; we can witness its origin yet daily. Give to a child a string, and he will soon call you to listen to the music he makes, by fastening it between the finger and the teeth, and then by increasing or diminishing its tension, produce higher or lower sounds. This is the principle upon which stringed instruments are constructed, and it is so simple, that their invention seems almost the first that must occur to men in pastoral life. The strings of different size and length, generally furnished by the bowels of animals, are attached to a piece of wood, a sounding board; and, in this manner, we have an instrument which, in its different forms, has been called, in ancient and modern times, either the lute, the lyre, the cithara, or the harp. Its origin must as little be sought among the Hebrews, the Egyptians, or the inhabitants of the fabulous Atlantides, as among the Scythians, Goths,[1] or Britons, but over all the world, among all people, and in all times. Montfaucon examined 600 different kinds of lyres, citharas, and harps, without being able to discover any peculiar and *national* differences.[2] Those learned treatises, there-

---

[1] See Pinkerton's *Enquiry*, Vol. i., p. 390.
[2] Montfaucon, *Antiq. Expl.*, Tom. iii., lib. v., cap. 3.

fore—those erudite historical researches about the climate, the people, or the century, which first gave birth and cultivation to music, are researches thrown away.[1] Music is as old as mankind, and has been invented by every people upon the globe. Wherever we find a people, however secluded or isolated, separated by sea or mountains from other people, there we find music and musical instruments. Every shepherd may be said to be its inventor. The reed on the moors, the little pipe cut from the tree, are the parents of flute, clarionet, oboe, and bassoon; the cow-horn is that of the horn, the trumpet, and the trombone; a hollow tree, pieces of slate, of iron, that of the instruments of percussion, drums, timbrels, and cymbals.

If we follow these observations one step further, we shall find, that, in proportion as musical skill progresses in the construction of the instrument, musical inspiration rises in the field of invention. The simple pastoral pipe must soon have become insufficient. He who possessed one, would feel that two or three connected together would produce more effect; for a primitive taste will seek effect in strength. Two or three pipes of different size were added to it; but there were only two hands to cover and uncover the holes of the one which was made to sing; therefore, each pipe would produce only one additional sound. There was, moreover, but one mouth for the additional pipes, so that a more powerful originator of wind was invented, in form of a bag; and thus we find again, among all nations of ancient and modern times, that pipe which is called the bagpipe. The contempt generally thrown upon this ungraceful child of antiquity, I do not participate in. This uncouth instrument, low as is its standard among the more perfect and more civilized means of communicating sound, has an interest of a manifold kind, and holds among popular instruments the first rank, as being one of the oldest and most universally known. The bagpipe, moreover, although a humble pastoral instrument in its ori-

---

[1] Some Scotch historians are puerile enough to say, that James I. of Scotland, others that Rizzio, were the inventors of the Scotch music.

gin, became a warlike instrument among the Romans,[1] and
is still so among the sons of ancient Caledonia. The bagpipe, limited in its mechanism, poor in its expression, is not,
on these accounts, deficient in the accents of joy and grief;
and no instrument has been a closer witness of heroic deeds;
none has ever found a warmer echo in warmer hearts!
Many pipers have died as heroes; the history of pipe-tunes
is the history of battles; and these are the bloody records
of the history of a country. The pipe deserves more than
any other its biographer. The interest it lacks in polite
society, it amply compensates for in popular life. Though
unfit for the drawing-room, it was not found unfit for the
field of battle. The piano and violin, which reign in the
former with a glorious and well-deserved supremacy, would,
under the thunder of the cannon, but miserably supply its
place. The principal merit of this instrument, however, remains to be told. Although one of the humblest and
coarsest, it is the parent of the grandest, the most magnifi-
cent, the most complete—the organ; not without reason called the wonder of art. The bag has grown into the bellows,
and two or three pipes into hundreds.[2] The principle upon
which the sounds are produced, is in both exactly the same.

Not only is the invention of musical instruments found
among all nations, but vocal music also belongs to man by
nature. The child even, when building its miniature palaces
of cards or erecting mountains and cities of sand, hums melodies never heard, never learned before, and invents, like
the inhabitant of the groves, unconsciously, its own little

[1] Procopius, Lib. ii., cap. 22. It was called *tibia utricularis* or *chorus,*
(from *corium,* skin), among the Romans; and ἄσκαυλος (see ασκαύλης,
the bagpiper, mentioned by Dio Chrysostomus) among the Greeks.
From the Italian *cornomusa,* the French call it *cornemuse* or *musette.*
The name *Bock* (he-goat), which the Poles give to this instrument, comes
from their using for the bag the skin of a he-goat, to which they leave
the head, with beard and horns attached.

[2] Upon a medal of Nero, we find a flute of Pan, a *Syrinx,* with a number of pipes growing gradually less, attached to bellows; exactly the di-
minutive organ, our organ in its infancy.—See *Dr Burney's History of
Music,* Vol. i., p. 501.

warbling tunes. When more advanced in age, the feelings and emotions which occupy the human breast find relief in song. We may hear the voice of the young shepherd of the Pyrenean, the Swiss, or the Tyrolean Alps, expressing in wild, irregular strains, the actual sentiment of his soul—his happy or his melancholy mood. What inhabitant of the South Sea Islands can be more unacquainted with music than he? and yet his voice may be heard morning and evening; and his notes are often answered from the distant rock by another voice; and, it may be, that before the snow drives the herds from the summer pastures, both singers have passed the precipices which separated them, and inhabit the same *Alma*.

Although circumstances and natural scenery change the manners and habits of life, man is the same every where. He seeks communication—he seeks sympathy; and when distance is wide—when precipices and rivers divide him from his fellow creatures, nature points out the same means: the modulation of speech will be replaced by the modulation of song. Even the lifeless voice of the echo, in seclusion and solitude, has charms; and where there is an ear to listen, and even where there is but an echo, there soon will be a voice to speak or to sing.

The tones of song are carried farther than those of speech. Ask of those thousand singers, of those men, women, and children, who, in the streets, sell the commonest objects of life, why they announce their approach to the inhabitants of the populous city by a chant instead of a short speech? Their voice must reach their customers, whether they be in kitchens, cellars, or attics; and, therefore, in all countries, and under all climes, they sing. Hence those thousand songsters, those innumerable different melodies, that strike you first when you enter a large city. Wherever you go, by day or night, you meet them at every turn. The doleful cry of the little chimney-sweeper in London—the argentine voice of the little Savoyard in Paris—penetrate, long before daylight, into the most hidden recesses of your alcove, and call you without mercy from your deepest, sweetest dreams, and, with a cruel monosyllable, destroy the enchanting gardens of Armida, through which you were borne as upon eagles' wings. The same may happen to you at Rome, at Naples, at St Petersburg, or in Rio Janeiro. Those who sell water in the streets of Paris, as they must be heard beyond the rolling thunder of carriages, and the sound must reach the sixth and seventh floor, have a cry, which much resembles a cry of distress—that of a man who, too late, calls over from one shore to the other for the ferry boat; or of one who, from the midst of the consuming flame, cries for a helping hand.[1] The Sakas in Mecca, who, with water, offer paradise and salvation to the passing pilgrims, sing, on the contrary, in a quiet, sacred strain, their *Sebyl Allah!*"[2] Necessity, the great teacher of man in all other things, is also his teacher in music. What the desires of the mind, its dispositions and feelings, leave unaccomplished, circumstances bring into being. The same that we observe daily around us, travellers and historians have told of the people of other hemispheres and other ages. Sailors in hoisting masts, masons in lifting huge stones, have special tunes to give uniformity to their exertions. The boatman, to relieve the monotonous movement of the oar, has his song likewise; and the little melodies of this latter are on every coast to be found, as well in Arabia as among the fishermen of the Feroe Islands, or the gondoliers of the Venetian lagunes. We must all be familiar with those tunes with which mariners facilitate their wearisome labour, and gain regularity of step in dragging their boats against the stream. The beautiful description which Ovid gives of this, we find still realized, after almost two thousand years, by all those who navigate on canals and inland rivers.[3] This may lead us to understand why, when

---

[1] See my Work, *Les Cris de Paris.* Paris: Chez Curmer.
[2] Burckhard's *Travels in Arabia.*
[3]   —— Hoc est cur . . . .
   Cantet et innitens limosae pronus arenae
   Adverso tardam qui trahit amne ratem.
   Quique ferens pariter lentos ad pectora remos,
   In numerum pulsa brachia versat aqua.
                          OVID. Lib. Trist. iv. 1.

Lysander destroyed the walls of Athens, he caused all the musicians of his army to play during the operation of the workmen. Chardin, in his Travels in Persia, says, that oriental nations cannot accomplish any work which requires great bodily exertion, without a regular noise of some kind." [1] Music, therefore, is natural to man. To man, in combat with toil, it is the handmaid of necessity; to man at rest and in abundance, it is a recreation. Among the former, it will always bear a rougher stamp, and will be characterized more by a strongly marked rhythm than by melody; among the latter, melody will predominate; and, as being in closer connection with the sentiments, will come more and more under the dominion of art. It would, therefore, be in vain were we to expect to hear, every where alike, regular and expressive melodies.

The music of a people depends upon their mental and moral development. The first impressions man receives are those communicated by the senses. From them he passes to those which are the result of reflection, and bear the stamp of a higher, a more intellectual nature. The life of a nation is the same as that of an individual; the nearer a man is to the state of nature, the more he is under the dominion of the senses. The advance a people may have made in civilization, may easily be determined by the means they use to awaken their feelings or to gratify them. Drums, and rude pipes, or whistles, are the instruments of a savage people; their songs are cries, shouts, and a sort of monotonous howling. The warrior and the hunter like horns, drums, whistles, bells, and every instrument that conveys sound to a distance, and produces noise, and, through it, excitement; but to the fisherman, the shepherd, music soon ceases to be mere noise;

[1] Burckhard, in his *Travels in Arabia,* makes many similar remarks. The Arabs or Persians, on their pilgrimage to Mecca, especially when navigating in boats, replace the want of instruments, by clapping their hands in a certain rhythmical movement. A French traveller says:—
" Les Arabes ne pouvent pas exécuter le plus léger travail qui exige un peu d'accord et d'ensemble, sans entonner de chants simples et monotons, qui ne laissent pas d'avoir une certaine harmonie. Il est rare qu'on voit passer une barque sur le Nil sans entendre chanter les mariniers."

they have no desire to be heard but from rock to rock, or from grove to grove, like the shepherds of Theocritus and Virgil.

Music extends itself with the circle of feeling, as language does with that of thought. As soon as it was possible to convey a sense, a meaning, a sigh, by a succession of sounds, music gradually bècame a language—the language of the soul, of its dearest emotions ; music became an Art.

II.

THE first effect that music produces is merely physical. Sounds strike the nerves of the ear, and make, according to their power, quality, character, roughness, or sweetness, analogous impressions upon our senses. Too powerful, too sudden strokes might occasion nervous convulsions, destroy the faculty of hearing, or even extinguish life. In the endless variety of organizations, an endless variety of sensations is awakened by one and the same sound. A delicate, sensitive ear is otherwise affected than that of a stronger, rougher nature. The tumult, the whistles, and the shrieks in which the latter delight, would throw the other into the highest state of alarm or discomfort. Hence the curious anecdotes of men who could not tolerate certain sounds, and who, on hearing particular instruments, became the subject of the most unaccountable nervous sensations, of which no other person was conscious. The beating of a drum produces in many persons a corresponding tremulousness in the chest. Some persons cannot refrain from weeping whenever they hear a certain note. J. J. Rousseau says, that he knew a lady who could not hear any kind of music without being seized with involuntary and convulsive laughter. The delicacy of the ear of Mozart was so great, that, without being modified by other instruments, he could not tolerate the sound of a trumpet. His father, who wished him to overcome this sensibility, took him one day by surprise with a violent blast of a trumpet. The boy shrieked, grew pale, and

fell senseless to the ground.[1] The monk of St Gallen tells
us of a woman, who, when she heard an organ for the first
time, was so transported with rapture, that she never reco-
vered from the effect, and died in consequence.[2] Certain
chords act in a peculiar manner upon some constitutions. Instances are known, where the second inversion of the perfect
chord causes feverish excitement; and a distinguished virtuoso
on the violoncello in Germany, cannot hear a composition in
the key of *B min.* without getting positively ill.[3] The effects
music produces upon the deaf born, and to whom the sense
of hearing has been restored, are extraordinary, though not
surprising. Often they feel oppression, short breath, trembling of the limbs, grow pale, or have a quick pulse, a burn-
ing face, headache, giddiness, and at last faint.[4]

Animals, as well as men, are accessible to the effect of
sound. It is generally admitted that the spider delights in
music, and that, like the large green lizard of Italy, it will
draw near and nearer to it. A blind man in Silesia, by
whistling a few notes, drew, as by enchantment, all the crabs
from their hiding-places to a certain spot, and had no trouble
in catching all that came within his hearing.[5] The musical
susceptibility of certain dogs is very remarkable. In the
year 1827, all Rome went to see a dog, who, every day,
marched at the parade, before the military band; in the
evening he was found sitting in the orchestra of the theatre
Della Valle; no one ever knew whence he came, or to whom
he belonged. Some dogs will whine at certain sounds of instruments; they are indifferent to some keys, and extremely
sensitive to others. Experiments have been made upon a
certain dog, in playing in different keys; *A maj.* made him
always uneasy, but a composition *in E maj.*, excited him so
much that, on one occasion, when the cruel experiment was
continued too long, the poor animal became furious, and died

  [1] *Biography of Mozart,* by Nissen.
  [2] See also, *Vie de Charlemagne,* par Gaillard, Tom. iii., p. 95.
  [3] *Encyclopædie der Tonkunst,* Vol. v., p. 71. Stuttgart.
  [4] Magendie's *Physiologie,* Vol. i., from p. 242.
  [5] See *Historia Morborum,* p. 567. Breslau, 1720.

in the most frightful convulsions.[1] Well known is the remarkable effect of music tried in Paris in 1798, upon elephants.

But sounds not only act upon the nerves of man and animals,
but even upon inanimate objects. Glasses, mirrors, china
vases, have been seen to vibrate and break at certain sounds
of the flute, and notes of the human voice.[2] We may witness the latter in cathedrals, where certain pipes of the organ
cause a shaking of the windows, walls, and pillars. A
powerful bass voice in the lower notes, has, in a limited space,
the same effect upon chairs and tables.

Bartolini, in his work *on the flutes of the ancients*, gives
the most curious facts on the variety of musical effect on objects and individuals. It would be a labour of hours to read
only the titles of books communicated in Forkel's *Litera-
tur der Musik*, and Sulzer's *Theorie der Schönen Künste*,
and written by scientific men of all nations, on the effect of
music in bodily and mental disease. It would be necessary
to begin with Aristoxenus and Euclid, and enumerate works
in all languages, down to Rousseau and Buffon.

We see from these simple facts, that the magical power of
music is not always attributed to its right cause. We are
too often inclined to ascribe to the talent, either of the composer or of the performer, the whole merit of the wonderful
effects produced. Undoubtedly, the power of talent and
genius in the melodious and harmonious combinations of
sound should be acknowledged ; but it must not be forgotten,
that there is in the nature of sound itself something mysteri-
ously affecting. A simple sound, by whatever physical cause
produced, similar to that which issued from Memnon's statue,[3]
or which is heard from Fingal's Cave at Staffa, excite in us,

[1] *Musical Gazette of Leipzig,* viii. Jahrgang, No. 26. Compare
Kausch's *Psychologische Abhandlung* über den Einfluss der Töne, und
insbesondere der Musik auf die Seele.

[2] See Bourdelot *Histoire de la Musique,* T. i., p. 51 ; comp. *Universal
Lexicon,* article *Musik,* Vol. xxii.

[3] The Colosse of Memnon issued, according to tradition, two sounds :
at the first ray of the sun, in the morning, the sound which was heard
was gay ; at the last ray, in the evening, it was plaintive. The sounds

with all their monotonous repetition, a something that either fills us with melancholy or with awe. At midnight, the repeated call of the sailor who sounds the depth, or the blast of a trumpet heard from a watch-tower or minaret, have in them something solemn and majestic. The evening bell of a village church, sounds cheering and hospitable to every ear, and vividly do its strokes bring back to our recollection, with the days of infancy, our birth-place, the place where we learned to know our first joy, our first sorrow ; for if certain sounds act on the nerves, those which remind us of the past, which express a sentiment and reveal a feeling, must have an effect of a higher kind upon the soul. It would be difficult to mark the limit where the operation upon the senses and that upon the soul begins or ends. These are mysteries which lie beyond the surface of our attainments, but of which we have, however, many indubitable proofs. Melodies which we heard in our childhood, a song—the poorest as music or poetry—if it bring to our mind recollections of earlier and happier times, if it remind us of places and occurrences, or more still of persons whose memory lies near to our heart, who can doubt that its effect will be powerful, and a thousand times more so, than a composition infinitely richer, more regular, more harmonious and scientific ? The *Rans des Vaches*, is originally nothing but a melody composed of the three notes of a chord, played by the shepherd upon the horn of a cow, and is scarcely more than a signal of the cowherd of the Alps ; hence its name *Kuhreigen* in German ; *Rans des Vaches* in French. Its charms, therefore, are not in its music, but in the recollections of home and infancy.[1] Its sounds, like those of *Erin-go-bragh*, or *Lochaber no more*,

were heard until the IV. cent. of our era, when Probus restored it, and thus probably destroyed the cause of the phenomenon.—See Letronne *Sur la Statue Vocale de Memnon*, Paris, 1833. Compare Anders *Sur la Statue de Memnon.—Gazette Musicale de Paris*, Vol. i.

[1] " On chercherait en vain dans cet air les accens énergiques, capables de produire de si étonnans effets. Ces effets, qui n'ont aucun lieu sur les étrangers, ne viennent que de l'habitude, des souvenirs de mille circonstances qui, retracés par cet air à ceux qui l'entendent, et leur rappelant

speak more strongly to the memory and the heart than to the ear. At these accents, as by enchantment, past years, with all their joy and sorrow, rise as from the tomb, and surround like phantoms the imagination of the exile. National airs are, in this respect, most deeply affecting, and volumes upon volumes might be filled with facts gathered in the Irish and Scotch regiments, in the American and Peninsular wars, in India and elsewhere, of their wonderful effect when heard in a foreign land. Soldiers and settlers feel, according to the character of the melody, raised to the utmost excitement, or moved to the deepest dejection. "We were at a ball," wrote a few days ago a young Scotchman, from one of the islands in the Pacific Ocean ; "we danced and were happy : when all at once, to please me, a Scotch tune was struck up. It seized me with such power, that I was quite overcome : I could stand it no longer, and was obliged to leave the company, in order to hide my tears and my emotion." How deeply a simple tune, heard in our youth, can strike into the recollection of the past days of our existence, is illustrated in a remarkable instance which happened in the Glasgow Lunatic Asylum, and which was told to the author by the very persons concerned in it. Some patients in the ladies' ward met in the evening in the room of the matron. They took tea, sang, and were cheerful. A Scotch song, however, disturbed the harmony of the party : it caused such violent emotion in one of the patients, that they were obliged to remove her from the company. The following day she came to see the matron, and said, "Do you know why I wept so much yesterday in hearing that song ? It reminded me of some circumstances of which I had long since lost all recollection." Gradually, in retracing step by step, occurrences and events of long-forgotten years, she came to a clear understanding and sound appreciation of

leur pays, leurs anciens plaisirs, leur jeunesse, et leur façon de vivre, excitent en eux une douleur amère d'avoir perdu tout cela. La musique alors n'agit pas precisément comme musique, mais comme signe commemoratif."—J. J. Rousseau, *Dictionaire de Musique*, art. *Musique*.

her own situation; and not many weeks passed before she was restored to health and to her family.

All these effects scarcely belong as yet to music in its highest acceptation. As an art, it moves in a loftier sphere; and owes, on the one side, nothing to the nerves, and on the other, nothing to remembrance. When out of the depth of imagination, and supported by the resources of science, a lofty idea appears, clothed in beautiful and analogous forms, perceptible to one of our senses,—then we have before us a work of art; not *mechanical* art, which tends to satisfy some material exigencies, or serves some practical purpose, but which, as a free creation, is sufficient for and in itself, which in its individual completeness reveals to us a lofty thought, or awakens and satisfies some intellectual interest. Art is the earthly symbol of the creative power—the divinity in man: its object is, the perfectibility of mankind—the embellishing, ennobling of human existence. Man is endowed with a triple nature; he can therefore not derive a true, a permanent enjoyment, from productions purely material; his moral and intellectual powers must equally be occupied, find nourishment and satisfaction.

In the range of fine arts, those which penetrate the deepest with the least material element, must stand the highest. Music and poetry, therefore, occupy the first place: the latter is the communicating medium of the mind; the former, of the soul. All other arts, painting, sculpture, architecture, are composed of grosser materials; of tangible, visible elements; of wood and of stone, of marble and of colour. They imitate living nature, but in them is no movement, no life, no action; all is at rest, all is quiet, all is death. In music and poetry there is actual life; there are accents of joy; there are sighs and tears; there is an ocean, with its calms and its passions, its restlessly going and coming tide: and all this action, all this life, is manifested in no representation of any outward object: they wield their power in untangible sounds, unembodied in any outward form, imperceptible to every eye. These two arts are born as twins; their etherial origin stamps them as inseparable: and in this double nature they

are the most popular of all arts, and as old as man. It is
this indefiniteness, this aerial nature of music, which makes
an analysis of it so difficult, and which is the reason that
mediocrity can risk a public exhibition in this, with much less
danger of detection, than it can in any other of the arts.
From the same cause, a good work will more easily escape attention, and will not always at first have that rank assigned to
it which it deserves. The disadvantage is greater still when
compositions purely instrumental are concerned, in which no
assistance from the language of poetry comes to aid the language of sound.

The more the cultivation of the mind approaches perfection, the more complete will be the development of the musical taste; and we recede in the same proportion from the
dry combinations of harmony, which are not animated by
any genius, as from the empty sounds of a melody, which
passes meaningless away. We will want compositions, in
which melody, harmony, and rhythm combine in beauty and
truth, and in which mind and understanding, imagination
and feeling, at the same time attract and satisfy.

We learn from the great masters, that the manly and energetic character, the power and originality of the man of
genius, do not manifest themselves in the employment of a
great material mass, any more than by the greatest number
of strokes on instruments of the greatest volume. We know
works in which all arms and windpipes are set in motion,
the trombones and drums thunder like artillery upon the
deafened and defenceless ear, yet, with all this, we find therein no music : how different from the gigantic power developed by a Palestrina, an Orlando Lasso, a Marcello, a Clari,
in *four*, in *three*, in *two* simple voices ! The great, the majestic, the imposing in art, are recognizable more in the
design than in the colouring, more in the conception, the
disposition and symmetry of the whole, than in the dispro-
portionate details. " Let us all learn from Händel," says
Beethoven, " to produce so great effects with so few means."
The degree of sensibility, of elevation of soul, and a creative
power, is, as it were, the distinctive mark of the artist,

which is stamped upon his work, and which raises it so high above ordinary ones. Men of taste will therefore seek the influence and power of music, in another region than that in which the greatest perfection in mechanical effects is alone admired. Composers or players who so excel, are not always, in our opinion, the greatest artists, nor the most deserving of the name. We require something more than dexterity, than skilful execution. Many artists have attained this sort of excellence, whom we find but little calculated to inspire us with the taste and the love of the beautiful. See the numerous musical prodigies that land from all parts, and multiply like ants. These applauded musical stars are a part of what might be expected from the favour with which mere mechanical effects are received. It is a mischief that has made great inroads in the domain of art: it moves on with a speaking trumpet, calling all to come around and admire it. We are tired indeed of that unmeaning noise which says nothing to the soul, of the difficulties surmounted by mere dexterity, and at expense of thought; of the artifices without number, which do nothing to initiate us in the true beauties of the most powerful of all arts. We know not what one day will become of music, if people allow themselves to be caught in those skilful snares by which mountebanks pass for musicians, and a masterpiece of skill and patience for a masterpiece of art. No better warning can be held out to the stream of corruption in which the real art of music seems to combat for breath and life, than in the simple, but energetic sentence pronounced by Rochlitz, one of its truest admirers and greatest judges :—" Down with musical composition that expresses nothing. If music is the language of our sentiments, that which expresses no sentiment cannot be music."

Without doubt it is capable of being embellished, by yielding at times to a more passionate development, and more scientific combinations ; only we must not confound the principle of the art with the means of enhancing its value. " Music," says Thibaut, " will not appear to us of divine origin, unless the sensations which it procures for us transport us into the ideal world; the composer who cannot attain this, is nothing but a mechanician or a journeyman."[1] In all the other arts, the work of the artist finds more easily its own place: its distinctive character is more easily recognized, its symbols are more visible in every aspect. Music, too fugitive, resembles a vision: it evaporates at the same moment that it appears; you only hear, as it were, the light rustling of its garment, the vibration of its wings, its accent of joy and grief, and you feel just as you do at the instant you awake from a dream; your heart palpitates, and you repeat, like an echo in the distance, the same sounds, the same accents. Here we may say what elsewhere has been applied to poetry: Music, "in its purest effect, is a wonder; and the belief in it a wondrous belief;"[2] or exclaim with Cicero, (*Rem videam, causam nescio,*) "The effect I see, the cause I cannot penetrate."

Our studies, our enquiries and researches concerning the science, the history, the philosophy of music, may, on account of its supernatural power, its universality, be summed up in the words of Bettina,[3] "I would fain know what music is; I seek it as a man would seek eternal wisdom."

O music! thou art the evening twilight of this world; thou risest high above our griefs and tears, until thy rays melt in the morning dawn of the eternal!

[1] *Ueber Reinheit der Tonkunst.*

[2] Die Poesie in ihrer reinsten Wirkung ist ein Wunder, und der Glaube an dieselbe ein Wunderglaube.—*W. Müller.*

[3] Göthe, *Briefwechsel mit einem Kinde.*

B

III.

HAVING observed the various effects of music upon our sensations, we might at once approach the question of its power, influence, and importance upon the education of youth; but we must for a moment look around us, and see if there are not physiological and psychological reasons in its favour. In examining our musical organs—the voice that produces sound and the ear that receives it—we are struck with amazement at the wonders of their construction. The cause of the beauty and charm of the human voice, its flexibility and character, differing in age, sex, and individual, as much as the faces of men from each other, and the ear, mysterious channel, through which sound penetrates and strikes with power and certainty the inward man, remain, as yet, undefinable enigmas which have escaped every analysis, and will perhaps continue to baffle human science and enquiry; yet, both are an inheritance of nature, a common gift which, with more or less delicacy, belongs to all mankind. This is an important fact which should not escape the friend of education; for, if education has any object in view, it must be to develope our natural dispositions and faculties, and bring them to bear upon our future mental and moral advancement. But the marvellous construction of the ear, and the equally marvellous effect of the voice, are not the only points to which we would wish to direct attention; there is in the nature of our senses, in the diversity of their action, another powerful argument in favour of the cultivation of music.

Taste, smell, and feeling, are inferior senses, the lowest in the scale, and scarcely ever capable of reaching beyond the mere animal nature. The highest refinement of these consists in a keener relish for some things, and dislike to others. Hearing and seeing—the ear and eye—although they act equally as physical organs, are, nevertheless, susceptible of a higher cultivation, and can be elevated and ennobled. They reveal themselves in awakening deeper sensations, and pass beyond the mere external man. These senses ennobled, are offended at whatever is low, trivial, and inharmonious, and only find enjoyment in dignity, beauty, and grace ; they are the link between the outward and the inward world of man. Through their medium, tastes and distastes will be keener in all that relates to order and harmony. At first they bear only upon objects of the physical world, yet soon they will penetrate into a more spiritual sphere, and seek what is morally excellent and beautiful. It is in this moral power of the eye and ear, that the necessity and importance of their cultivation must be sought. Nothing in education can be substituted for the refinement and taste conveyed to man through the fine arts. Science developes and enlarges certain mental faculties, seeks physical results from physical causes, builds upon matter and fact ; in the one the anatomical knife, in the other the chemical apparatus, in a third the arithmetical figure, are the starting points ; armed with these weapons, men of science form their theories, their systems and hypotheses, and reach, one after another, in the world of intellect, to great results and great discoveries. How often has this been attained at the expense of all other faculties! giants in intellect and reasoning, in analysing, dissecting, and compounding, but with no heart, no humanity, nothing which reveals the nobler attributes, the higher destiny of man. Instruction of the mind has been erroneously taken for training and education. The mind, therefore, has been enlarged, but the man has been left in his infancy. To such there is but one temple, that of reality. That which cannot be measured with the compass, which cannot be proved by figures, does not exist. For him there is no power but steam, no ties which link man to man, but railroads. But too often he neither believes in virtue nor justice; history and philosophy, in short, the most vital, the most affecting questions of the thinking man, are to him objects of derision and ridicule. Art and literature have no greater enemies than such half-instructed,

half-educated men, commonly called men of science. It is
they who, after the performance of a work of a Händel or a
Beethoven, the reading of a Milton or a Shakespeare, would
ask, with the mathematician, after he had listened to the
reading of a Homer, what does this prove ? [1] What is poetry, what is art in general, to so cold and coarse a nature,—a
calculating machine, a living engine ? Stop the wheel of
the machine, let out the steam of the engine, and both will
resemble a bagpipe with a hole in its bellows.

The object of the fine arts, of poetry and music especially,
is man, man in his moral being, in his deepest and loftiest
thoughts and aspirations. They reach and penetrate, in
a manner peculiar and admirable, into the hidden recesses
of that being, and, by their influence and sympathy, warm
and stimulate it with a purifying flame, shield it from con-
tamination, and shed a lustre and beauty over the duties it
is called upon to perform. We may learn from without, from
general instruction to do what is right and just, because it
is a duty or a law, which under certain penalties we may not
transgress ; but he who is really accomplished, does what is
good and just, not only because it is a duty, but because it is
an imperative necessity of his more refined nature. In doing
otherwise, he would violate that nature, destroy that grace
and harmony with which his soul is filled, and place himself
in opposition with his more generous, his nobler self.

It remains now to be seen whether it is the eye or the ear
which operates most powerfully upon man, and which of
them leaves the deepest impressions. The mere sight of suffering can make the chords of our pity and compassion vibrate
powerfully ; but the broken sounds which acute pain, or
poignant grief, wring from the breast of the unfortunate,
touch us more deeply. Sounds have a hidden force, and

---

[1] Well may be applied to music and all other arts, what Rousseau so
well says in regard to Homer : " Les autres poètes écrivoient, dit-il, Ho-
mère seul avoit chanté ; et ces chants divins n'ont cessé d'être écoutés
avec ravissement, que quand l'Europe s'est couverte de barbares qui se
sont mêlés de juger ce qu'ils ne pouvoient sentir."—*Essai sur l'Origine
des Langues*, chap. VI.

the impressions which are made through the sense of hearing, are more lively and thrilling than those which only affect the organ of sight. Leibnitz says (*Picturæ explicatiores, soni fortiores*):—" Painting explains better, but sounds have more power." It is only the outside, the surface of things, which is accessible to the eye. " The ear," says Herder, " penetrates the deepest, and affects more powerfully than any sense, the whole nervous system." In the description of exterior nature, of all that is measurable and limited by space, music is totally powerless, and yields the supremacy to painting and the plastic arts ;[1] but where the interior life, the sensations of man, are to be moved, music stands the first ; its effects are the most striking, the most immediate. A mixture of colours, without harmonious arrangement, may offend the sight ; but discordant, powerful, and unexpected sounds, can so affect the ear, that every nerve suffers, and is deeply shaken. Painting can touch, can charm, can elevate, but music makes the heart thrill with delight, and fills the soul with rapture. There exists a most intimate and a most mysterious connection between the vibrations of the air and those of the heart ; every external sound finds there an echo ; every appeal a reply; mirth and sadness, pity, hope and remembrance, affection in all its phases of joy and grief, find a vibrating string in that harp of divine workmanship—the human soul. In this secret relation between sense and feeling, the

[1] A *school* has lately risen in France, in which imitation of external nature, description of events and accidental occurrences, are represented in music. Not only audible, but visible nature, *high* and *low*, *white* and *black*, clouds, rivers, mountains, and precipices, are painted by musical sound. At the first glance it must appear evident how little connection musical description or painting can have with real art. In the midst of the many enthusiastic admirers of the so called *fantastic* school, it has found the appreciation it deserves among men of more refined taste. A French writer says on the performance of the *Shakespeare symphonie* of *Romeo et Juliette* :—" In the midst of a tumult of horns and double basses, I wanted to know the signification of it : I looked into the descriptive programme, and found the words, ' The gardens of Capulet, SILENT and DESERTED.' I read there too, he continues, ' *Romeo sentait les premières atteintes du poison.*' Les violons ont fait entendre un bruit strident ; un admirateur enthousiaste s'est écrié : *comme c'est bien cela la colique!* ' "

nerves and their corresponding sensations, lies the mystery and the power of music. By adapting the melodious inflections of the voice, their character, tone, and colour, to the sentiment which we intend to express, we govern, with an almost supernatural force, the human breast, and produce in thousands, at the same moment, the emotions which we individually felt, or wished to call forth. No art can wield with such admirable suppleness the most delicate movements of the soul, or be made to pourtray so vividly the most indefinable and mysterious sensations. No; no art has ever exercised over the human breast so decided an empire.

Thus we see that the cultivation and refinement of our senses is not so trifling an object in education as it might appear, and that the outward and the inward man, whose messengers they are, are intimately linked together, give and receive impressions; that neither without the other can rise or fall; that when the one ascends the scale of perfectibility, the other cannot remain in constant infancy.

He who is inaccessible to music, is defective in the harmony of his senses, is deprived of the nobler faculties which elevate man above the brute. Let him then boast of his unmusical nature, his unpoetical ear, his dislike or indifference to any of the fine arts; he has characterized himself; he has pronounced his own sentence. Shakespeare has left a monumental epigram to him who has "no music in his soul:" he may try in vain to efface it, it will stand and be true to the end of time.[1] Of what lofty, what exalted enjoyments he is deprived, those only know who have drank from the celestial fountain hours of happiness and rapture. In the enjoyment of works which, in thought and form, are congenial to us, we rise beyond this world, place an im-

---

[1] " We can only sing songs," says Luther, " with a pious, good, and cheerful heart; it is impossible to sing, at least any thing good, in the presence of a dull or bad man." A Roman cardinal expresses Luther's and Shakespeare's thoughts with a little more dogmatical emphasis, and abandons such men, without ceremony, to the devil, because he and his like hate all harmony. " Qui musicam non callet, seu nullo oblectamento animi illam audit, ex diabolo est, nam solus ille omnem harmoniam respuit."

mensity of space between the physical and spiritual part of ourselves; we are transported, as Schiller says, " to the spheres of the gods." We live a soul-existence, in unattainable exclusiveness from all that is earthly. This immersion into the ocean of thought and feeling, is the noble privilege of man; it is the seal of his higher destiny, and can, therefore, not be traceless in its passage. Called to ourselves from the inward to the outward world, reminded of our cares and our wants, has no impression followed us thither? Have we left the ideal world in which we lived, no matter how long, how short a time, at the threshold of this? Impressions of so sublime a kind are not so easily effaced. Their traces will still be found in the daily transactions of life. Where there is light, there is shadow; man stands between both; the shadow he casts upon the sand, is a representation of himself—the object lighted from above. A man, susceptible of lofty thoughts, deep, pure feelings, holy raptures, with a soul open to truth in music, to beauty in poetry, will, in daily life, not be forsaken by his better self.

When we, therefore, look upon the mysterious origin of music, the unaccountable effects of the voice, and the sensitiveness of the ear, its wonderful operation between the external nature and the internal man, between our senses and our soul, the universality of its language, its application to all ages, all nations, and all climes, to every individual in all stages of civilization and society, then we must exclaim, that there is a deep sense, a deep philosophy in music; that it might be a powerful auxiliary in directing the destiny of the human family. This should be done in schools, where the boy prepares and arms himself for the school of life and endurance; where, between mirth and play, he advances unconsciously towards the days of combat and adversity. Arm him, then, with all that is great, true, and beautiful. Teach him to think and to feel. Arm him with knowledge, with science! above all, arm him with art! and what is art, but the unchangeably, the eternally beautiful! It stands a faithful friend by our side in active life, and whispers warning to our soul in silent solitude.

IV.

HAS music really degenerated ? has it lost the magic power it once possessed ? Where are then the miracles equal to those with which ancient history is so filled ? And, is music worth acquiring, if it has fallen from its former throne, and if, in the course of ages, it has lost its charm, its power aud grandeur ? These are the usual remarks, to which every one gives his own conclusions, more or less based upon sound judgment and attentive observation. Music, in its effects, is the same now as it was, and will be so to the end of time. If we examine all those melodies which have produced extraordinary effects upon individuals, upon multitudes or nations, and thus have acquired historical importance, we shall find that their power is not derived from science or artistical combination, but is founded in truth, nature, and simplicity. These are the great engines of influence in musical composition and performance. It is a power more frequently found in melodies of popular and instinctive origin, than in works of art ; or, if met with in the latter, it is because those same qualities are predominant. In the scientific and difficult, the musician, the composer, as well as the performer, will be admired ; but it is by his simplest strains that he will captivate and subdue his hearer, that he will reach his deeper affections. Whenever we find a melody in the mouth of a whole nation, whenever an air is heard that produces strong feelings of excitement or despondency, we may be certain that it stands away from the refinements of art, and is powerful in its effects in proportion to its simplicity. To this must be added the constant association of the two sister arts, poetry and music. What in the language of music is too vague, too indefinite, acquires, through poetry, its real character, form, and colour. All poets of antiquity were musicians. Music without poetry, poetry without music, were things unknown. If ancient music had any advantage over ours, it was owing to the intimate union of both. The poet-musician was of a higher cast: what music wanted in thought, it received from the poet: what to poetry was unattainable in feeling, charm, and transport, the musician supplied in his turn. Music is more poetical than poetry itself: where words are inadequate to an overwhelmed bosom, be it in joy or grief, where poetry stands at its extreme limits, where excessive feeling strikes the stammering tongue with helplessness, there music begins to rise, and opens, with unequalled, with magic power, the gates of the wonderful, the celestial, and the infinite. In the superiority of the Grecian poets consisted, and therein only, the superiority of the Grecian music. Homer, and all the early bards of Greece, were not only poets, but musicians and singers. Such was Hesiod; such also were Sappho and Alcæus, the two children of Lesbos. How beautifully significant is Horace's ode on the effect of the singing of Sappho and Alcæus in the Orcus, when he says: " they were worthy of the sacred silence that surrounded them ; the multitude, filled with admiration, approached nearer and nearer, until shoulder pressed on shoulder."[1] At the side of Sappho, in the poetical world, the most splendid star of antiquity, Pindar, was a musician, and the son of a musician of Thebes. Æschylus, Sophocles, Euripides, the glorious triumvirate of ancient tragedy, were not only the poets, the musical composers and choreographers, (χοροῦ διδάσκαλοι) but even the musical performers of their dramas. Who then can understand the ancient Grecian poets, deprived of half their attributes ? Although the melodies have been lost to us, yet there is an ideal music in them, without which no scholar will pretend to understand their full poetical worth, far less their metrical and rhythmical cadence and melo-

---

[1] " Densum humeris bibit aure vulgus."—Od., Lib. xi. 13.

dy. The chorus is the mother of the Grecian tragedy, and the ideal of the Grecian popular and national songs. But who can approach them without music? or can, perhaps, a translation, the most successful translation of a Voss, a Müller, a Tieck, or a Schlegel, of a Shakespeare or a Pope, give us a distant idea of that musical charm, that poetical perfume which intoxicates us in ancient poetry? Approach it in its native garb, in its Greek idiom and Greek costume, or it closes, like the sensitive flower, its bosom and its charms. It is the Greek language, the melody of its lines, which gives you a distant foreboding of its music. Music and poetry are here like the two birds which have but one life; separate what has been born inseparable, and both will die.[1]

Without entering thus into the spirit of classical art and literature, without nourishing our soul with the beautiful of which they are so replete, and of which they are such perfect and inimitable models, classical studies are nothing worth. What avails it to know the Latin and Greek alphabet, grammar, and syntax, and to have approached, as a stammering schoolboy, some of the easy classics of either nation? If this is what you call classical education, you are right to say that you do not see (and who would say the contrary?) what connection music has with Greek. When schools and universities do not reach beyond the grammati-

---

[1] Herder says about the music in Pindar's Odes: " We stand like in the stream of Tantalus; and as the musical stream flows hence, we seek in vain to grasp the golden fruit."—*Stimmen der Völker in Liedern.* vol. vii.

In speaking of *popular songs, ancient ballads,* and especially that of Shakespeare's *Twelfth Night*—

Come away, come away death,

he says, as beautifully as truly : " Let such lines be translated, how different will they appear, even in regard to their sentiment, when you take away all its external attributes or form in tone and melody, all that mysterious and indescribable something, which, with music, stream-like fills our soul! (*was uns mit dem Gesange stromweise in die Seele fliszt.*) Open the relics of ancient poetry, translate any thing you like, and as beautifully as you may, but without the musical accent, the melody,— and see then what remains."—*Ibid.*

cal analysis of Greek poetry, then poetry itself is, and must
remain, an unknown land; far more so still, the indis-
pensible sister attribute, the music of their poetry. You
flatter yourself and your schools by calling them classical;
but the classical consists not in the grammar, it consists in
literature and art. Instead of giving to your students (to use
the bombastical style of some church writer,) a *glance at the
temple*, instead of making them Peripatetics in its portico,
and allowing them to look through the key-hole, throw the
gates open, and lead them into the sanctuary, that there
they may drink at its source the knowledge of classical art,
which, like a sacred fire, will purify their thoughts, elevate
their taste, refine their manners, embellish their life, imbue
them with the laws of order and harmony, and render them
better and wiser in life and action. " Grecian art is a school
of mental refinement, (*Humanität*); a poor man is he who
does not regard it as such."[1]

Was Grecian music more powerful, because we read that
rocks and forests followed the singer, that walls, temples,
and cities rose at the sound of his voice and lyre? Icelandic
chronicles tell us the same of Scandinavian mythology almost in the same words: " Odin excelled all men in the art
of poetry, eloquence, and music, and could sing airs so tender
and melodious, that even rocks would expand with delight,
while the spirits of the infernal regions stood motionless

[1] " Die Griegische Kunst ist eine Schule der Humanität; unglücklich
ist wer sie anders betrachted."—Herder, *Die Humanität der Griechen*,
vol. xv.

Through the influence of classical literature upon refined education, the languages—Greek as well as Latin, and all other studies
which lead to it—were called *studia humaniora*, or *humanitatis*, and,
lastly, *humanity*, which expression is in England erroneously given to
Latin alone. If, for their polishing and refining influence sake, the
classical studies are not called humanity, we do not understand its meaning. There is certainly very little humanity in *us, a, um*, and quite as
little in τύπτω, τύπτεις; and it is without doubt, that humanity is to be
roused in the education of boys, whom even Plato called the most un-
manageable of all animals, ὁ παῖς πάντων θηρίων ἐστὶ δυσμεταχειρισ-
τότατον; which Ficinus elegantly translates with—*Puer omni bestia
intractabilior*.

around him."[1] When Orpheus sang, the oak had an ear,
Ixion's wheel stood still, and the Danaides forgot their endless toil.   This all tells of the wonderful effects produced by
music, and the works that were achieved through its aid.
Take away the allegoric garb, and you will find that the poet-
musician was no less than the instructor and benefactor, the
legislator of cities and provinces.   Through the charm of
poetry and music, he acquired among savage tribes an attentive ear, sang of great men and great deeds, inspired them
with a love for the good and the just, for virtue and order.
Through his power of eloquence and fascinating musical nar-
ration, they erected walls, cities, and temples, submitted themselves to the laws they had listened to, and had learned to
love and to sing.[2]   Similar effects were produced with similar
elements among nations of other climes.   "Who is not acquainted with the miracles of the bards and the scalds ? with
the marvellous effects produced by the troubadours and minstrels ? how the eager people gathered around them, and
what a new world was opened to their sight ?   How sacred
were those songs in which the people learnt the history, the
traditions, and with them, the language and manners of their
nation ! They were simple but powerful, full of energy and
action : they were an appeal to the heart, and by the severity
of their accents, became a piercing dart to the soul open to
truth."[3]

We have a faint echo of the songs of ancient Israel and
ancient Greece, in those which the Christian Church borrowed

---

[1] Snorris *Heimskringla*, and Mallet's *Northern Antiquities.*

[2] The laws of Greece, as well as those of all ancient nations, were sung.
Aristotle says : " Why have we in Greece no other word for *law* than
νόμος ? (song.) Was it because, when writing was as yet unknown,
they sang the laws, that they might not be forgotten, as it is still the
custom among the Agathursi ?"

Διὰ τί νόμοι καλοῦνται οὕς ἄδουσιν ; ἢ ὅτι πρὶν ἐπίστασθαι γράμ-
ματα ἦδον τοὺς νόμους, ὅπως μή ἐπιλάθωνται· ὥσπερ ἐν ʼΑγαθύρσοις
ἔτι ἐιώθασι ;—Arist. *Probl.* xix. 28.

[3] Herder's *Lieder der altrn Voelker*, vol. vii.

from both, and transmitted to us in the Greek and Roman
Churches, by written and oral tradition. The Antiphones,
hymns and psalms, are remains of Grecian and Hebraic music.
Both lived for nearly two thousand years in the mouth of the
eastern and occidental nations, and still they stand before us
living monuments of piety and enthusiasm, models of simplicity, truth, and grandeur. These sacred hymns and psalms
were for ages popular melodies of all Christian nations : they
resounded in dungeons and catacombs, and accompanied man
from the cradle to his grave. Their simplicity is such, that
often they have no more notes than syllables, and with all
this, who can hear without emotion, the " *Te Deum Lauda-
mus*" of Ambrose, or the funeral song, " *Jam moesta quiesce
querela*" of Prudentius, both productions of the fourth century ? The *Pange Lingua*, the *Veni Redemptor gentium*, the
Veni Creator, were for centuries the war songs of the French
armies.[1] After Charlemagne, it was the song of Roland
(Cantilena Rolandi) that inflamed them with enthusiasm.
Among the Slavish nations it was St. Adelbert's Hymn, the
Boga Rodziça, which resounded in every church and upon
every field of battle.

Music at all times has seen its miracles : A song—the
poorest as music or poetry—if it bring back recollections of
earlier or happier times, if it remind us of places and occurrences, or of persons whose memory lies near to our heart,
who can doubt that its effect will be powerful, and a thousand times more so than a composition infinitely richer, more
regular, more harmonious, and more scientific would be !
The singing of the Jewish captives may have been little more
than the rhythmical and melodious recitation of a psalm, yet
the Babylonian soldiers liked to listen to those songs of Zion,
which overwhelmed with grief and tears the exiled children
of Israel. The choruses in the Grecian tragedies, which
consisted in a monosyllabic recitation, a melodious and
rhythmical declamation, rising and falling, growing and diminishing in power and expression, simple, but true in thought

---

[1] *Chapelle-Musique des Rois de France*, par Castile-Blaze, p. 32.

and form; yet what terror did they not produce in the
Eumenides of Æschylus, and what tears in that touching
farewell scene of Euripides Alcestis! After the taking of
Athens by Lysander, one of the Thebans proposed, that
Athens should be destroyed, and all the citizens deprived of
their liberty. While the leaders of the enemy's army were
celebrating their victory in the banquet hall, one of the guests
sang the melody of the chorus of Euripides, " *O daughter of
Agamemnon, Electra, I come to thy humble dwelling.*" So
great was the emotion, the feeling of compassion which it
excited among the listeners, that it saved Athens from destruction, and the citizens from servitude.[1]

The wonders which the ancients attributed to music, although related by the greatest historians and philosophers,
we are much inclined to take for fables, for " Tales of a
Thousand and One Nights." But do not our own days tell
us of similar wonders achieved by this art? If ancient history relates that Timotheus could, according to the choice of
his melody, excite or calm Alexander's soul; that Tirtæus
was able to inflame for death or victory the Spartan army;
have we not instances near our own times of similar effects?
effects, indeed, which stand in nothing behind the reputed fables of antiquity. In the fifteenth century, in Granada, did
not the whole mass of the people shed tears when they heard
the ballad of the Moors, on the taking of Alhama? did not
the simple and pathetic song of Schah-Culi, at the siege of
Bagdad, save the life of 30,000 inhabitants?[2] Was not, a
century ago, the *Rans des Vaches* forbidden, under pain of

---

[1] Plutarch's *Life of Lysander.*

[2] When Amurat IV. conquered Bagdad in 1638, he gave orders to
massacre before his eyes, 30,000 inhabitants. Schah-Culi found means to
be brought before the irritated Sultan, and in singing to the harp the la-
ment of the suffering Bagdadians, Amurat was moved to tears; the massacre, already commenced, was countermanded. In softening this blood-
thirsty tiger with his strains, still sung among the Turks and Persians,
and known under the name of *Muselie* or *Percerfi Bagdati Fetichi,* (the
taking of Bagdad,) he is deservedly called the Persian Orpheus.—See To-
derini on the *Literature of the Turks,* and *Encyclopädie der Musikali-
schen Wissenschaften,* Vol. vi., p. 160.

death, because, to the memory of the sons of Switzerland, serving far away from their country, it recalled their native hills so powerfully, as to make them desert their ranks, or die of grief? Have we not witnessed the *Marseillaise Hymn*, wherever it was heard, exciting indescribable enthusiasm : the workmen quitting their shops, abandoning wife and children, and running in their shirt-sleeves to swell the ranks of the republican army? Deeds, which seemed beyond human power, were accomplished whenever the Marseillaise was struck up:[1] and even at this moment its power is electric upon the French; its intonation still strikes with awe and terror the most valiant armies of royalty. It is, therefore, kept in constant thraldom; always feared, always watched like a lion ready to break forth from its den, and spread, a second time, desolation and carnage over half the nations of Europe. Similar effects were produced by the *Polonaise of Kosciuszko* and the *Third May* in the combat of Poland for independence ; similar enthusiasm excited among the Neo-Hellenists the Δεύτε παῖδες τῶν Ἑλλήνων ; similar excitement produces daily still the *Gamel Norge* among the Norwegians. For the same reason, the nursery song has often a power over our feelings, that no work of musical genius could attain. J. J. Rousseau, when speaking of his aunt Suzon, when a child, says :—" Would one believe, that an old dotard, like myself, worn out with cares and troubles, should find myself weeping like an infant, while I murmur, with a broken and trembling voice, the songs of my childhood." [2]

It is known that the aria, *Ombra adorata aspetta* of Zingarelli's *Romeo e Giulietta*, so remarkable for its simplicity, caused an unheard-of emotion : as in the Eumenides of Æschylus, many people fainted, and women were carried away. Carpani relates,[3] that when Bertoni's opera, *Arta-*

---

[1] The words of the Republican General are known, who asked for a " supply of 1000 men, or a new edition of the Marseillaise ;" or another, who reported : " J'ai gagné la bataille ; La Marseillaise commandait avec moi."

[2] *Confessions de J. J. Rousseau.*

[3] Carpani's *Biography of Haydn.*

xerxes, was being performed in Rome, the character of Arbace was represented by a celebrated singer. At the famous judgment scene, the maestro had introduced some pauses to the instrumental accompaniment, after the words, *E appur sono innocente!* The action, the music, the art, and expression of the singer, had transported the whole audience. After these touching words, Arbace, perceiving the continued silence of the orchestra, turned round to the conductor, with somewhat of temper, and said : well, what are you all about ? who, recalled to himself, replied : we weep. In truth, audience and orchestra, carried away by the power of his expression, remained mute and motionless, listened and wept.

In many instances, when misfortune has struck too deeply into the heart, and ravaged, with little mercy, its dearest affections, when all the energies have been paralyzed, and tears, that great source of comfort, dried up, music has often come in unexpected, simple, touching strains, and presented a balm which medical science sought for in vain, a balm which, with its invisible source, appeared to be administered by an angel of comfort, a messenger from higher spheres.[1]

Thus we see that simple compositions have at all times operated more powerfully upon individuals and people than complicated scientific compositions ; and, therefore, it can be nothing but idle speculation to pretend that, in modern times,

---

[1] In the year 1778, the celebrated singer, Raff, came to Naples, where resided, at that time, the Princess Belmonte Pignatelli, who, brooding over her grief at the loss of her husband, had fallen into a state of total insensibility and stupefaction, and was fast approaching the grave. No tear brought relief to the breaking heart ; medical skill had been tried in vain. In this extremity of desolation, her waiting woman, as a last resource, arranged that, while seated one evening in one of her summer houses, Raff should sing, as by chance, from a distance. He, with an unpretending voice, sung that simple melody of Rolli, *Solitario bosco ombroso*. The Princess seemed at first insensible, but soon the head rose ; she opened the half-closed eyes, gazed as if awaking from a dream, and scarcely had Raff finished the first verse, when, fully conscious, she burst into a flood of tears, which continued for several days uninterruptedly. Thus her life was saved, and her spirits, by degrees, recalled to their former energy.—See Schilling's *Encyclopædie der Tonkunst*, art. *Raff*.

music has either no longer that wonderful power which it had among the ancients, or that their music was then in its infancy, compared with the more harmonious and the more scientific development of ours. The power of music is still undiminished; its application to youth, and to the people, has only to be learnt.

As simple music, then, produces the greatest effect, why should not every one find an opportunity to learn it?—In order to make the instruction in this art a really moral instruction, a powerful agent in the advancement and progress of individuals and nations, let us associate the simplest music with the best and noblest lines of poetical composition. Let us, with songs and poetry, with lessons of lofty thought and practical truth, store the memory of the young. What we are taught to sing, we never forget. The songs which we learnt in our youth, are the sweetest and most lasting recollections of man.

V.

Music among the Ancients, an essential part of Education.—Estimation in which Music was held by the Egyptians and Hebrews, by the Sages, Legislators, and the Founders of the different Schools of Philosophy in Greece.

THE music of the ancients, their technical acquirements, their scientific principles of this art, are to us a great mystery. Hundreds of years have passed since the last strains of their music were heard. In vain we listen to their songs of praise or of triumph, of hope or of contrition ; in vain we seek for them among their ruins, their temples, and their monuments ; these sounds are hushed ; they are gone to the grave with those who sought in them delight and comfort. The most minute and the most learned treatises have been written on the subject, but they leave us in the dark as we were before. No description, no explanation can help us. Sounds, sounds we want, living sounds carried upon the breath of man, or a notation of which we possess the key ; a writing in accordance with our measure, our musical compass, to be our guide through the infinity of auditive space. One canto of a Rhapsodist, one stanza of the Paeans, one scolion, one ode of Sappho or of Pindar, in its musical accents, would reveal to us the nature of the Grecian music. The only

Φράζου λάβε, λάβε, λάβε,

the terrible cry of the awakening furies in Æschylus' Eumenides ;[1] one strophe of their invocation *to the Night*,

Μᾶτερ ἅ μ᾽ ἔτικτες, ὦ μᾶτερ
Νύξ,[2]

would give us more insight into the music of the Grecian tragedies, than the investigations of many centuries have been able

---

[1] V. 125.　　　　[2] *Eumenides,* v. 312.

to accomplish. But with the nations, to a great extent, disappeared their monuments of history, their monuments of art; some temples only, some statues, escaped the general destruction, and a limited portion is left to us of Greek and Roman literature. Of the Phœnicians, no direct tradition has survived the storm of time. Of the Egyptians, nothing but their obelisks, pyramids, and a few hieroglyphics. Of that people, called the holy people, the people of God, a nation of priests, of their history, their poetry, their music, we know only what can be gathered from those fragments contained in the holy scriptures, and in the writings of the Talmudists.

What, then, is it that remains for us to tell about the music of the nations of antiquity? of their music as science, its technical principles and development? Almost nothing. The only point of which we can speak with certainty, in which we stand upon firm ground and have nothing to fear from future theories, is, that the ancients had a music, a music full of effect and power; that it was associated with every festivity of public and private life, with the laws and the religion of their country; that it was studied, honoured, recommended by their legislators, by the wisest men of all nations; and that it formed a part of moral cultivation, a branch of the education of youth. Egypt has been the cradle of the arts and sciences. The Greeks and Hebrews were only its disciples. It must certainly be a most interesting question, how music was appreciated by a people so renowned for their wisdom as the Egyptians. To their schools came the learned, the philosophers, the lawgivers of all nations. In them Moses was educated;[1] there studied Solon[2] and Pythagoras there learned philosophy, the political and sacred sciences. Plato passed there thirteen years of his life. In regard to the Egyptians, therefore, we may say with Cicero: " Audiamus enim Platonem quasi Deum Philosophorum."[3] Plato makes frequent usage of their principles of government, and

[1] Strabo, lib. xvi.   Philo, *De Vita Mosis*, lib. i.

[2] Plato, *Symposium.*   Plutarchus, Συμποσιακῶν, p. 153.

[3] Cicero, *De Natura Deorum*, lib. ii.

presents them often as a model to Greece, namely, in regard
to music. In their general outlines, they might be still a
model to us ; and if ever again music is to be earnestly, carefully and successfully applied to education, then what the
Egyptians did in the education of the young, what Plato ad-
vises the statesmen of Greece to imitate, must again become
a reality to us. Though we may have little to learn from the
ancients in the mechanical art, yet in practical wisdom, in
the philosophy of life, they might be still our masters. They
have been so in our religion, and until this hour the disciples
and priests of Memphis[1] are our masters, our high priests,
our prophets ; and their doctrines are our doctrines, their
laws our laws. The fine arts were cultivated in Egypt, and
applied to the education and the refinement of the people.
Greece followed its example, improved them, and carried to
its last limits their perfection. If we acknowledge the works
of the Greeks as the highest models of art, why not learn
from them the application of art for the furtherance of the
welfare, the mental and moral culture, the happiness of men
and of nations ?   In reading Plato's *Laws* and *Republic*, we
find that it was the opinion of the first legislators of Egypt,
that to render man happy in society, his sentiments of pleasure and pain must be regulated, that his feelings and expressions of joy and sorrow must be subjected to moderation.
Convinced also that the feeling of delight experienced by
music and rhythm, was as a divine blessing given to man, as
a means to cure or to prevent passions or vice, the source of
all evil, so destructive to individual or social harmony, they
sought for songs and dances, in which the noblest expressions
of the voice were united with the most dignified, the most
graceful movements of the body. The songs and dances were
intended to express the mental state of the wise, the virtuous,
the temperate ; and by means of poetry, melody, and rhythm,
they sought to inspire the young with the love of courage
and moderation.[2]

---

[1] Strabo calls Moses a priest of Egypt : Μώσης γάρ τις τῶν Αἰγυπ-
τίων ἱερέων.—STRABO, lib. xvi. p. 760.

[2] That ὄρχησις, as a branch of education, or as a part of Grecian tra-

Music was regarded as subordinate to poetry, and the poet-musician was subject to a great penalty, if his writings had any other tendency, than to excite an admiration of what was good and virtuous. Education with them consisted in the art of guiding the young towards what the law, in conformity with reason, had recognized as good, and what had been acknowledged as such by the oldest and the wisest of the nation. To be ignorant of music and dancing, signified with them to be ignorant how to moderate and to regulate words and actions: they united the good with the useful; dancing and grace were inseparable; and a man was only then considered accomplished, when he was in full possession of these united qualifications.

Moses, educated as a child of Pharaoh, learned from the Egyptians, according to Philo and Clemens of Alexandria, arithmetic, geometry, and *all the branches of music*, viz. rhythm, metre, harmony, its theory, and its practical application to the voice and to instruments.[1] Throughout the whole of the Scriptures, we find that music was an inseparable companion of the Israelites, in joy and grief, in private and public festivities: in sacred rites, priests, prophets, and kings sang and played on instruments, with the

---

gedy, cannot mean jumping or leaping like fawns, monkies, and satyrs, or like the drunken worshippers of Dionysos, as Mr G. H. Lewis, (see *Classical Museum*, vol. II. p. 344,) or Bishop Blomfield, (*Museum Criticum*, vol. II.) would make us believe, is evident from every line in which it is mentioned as such. If the tragic dance was something else than lofty movement, majestic carriage, and graceful step, regulated by musical rhythm, how is to be explained the dancing in the religious festivities mentioned in the biblical writings? The movements of the "*old men figuring up and down the stage*," as his Lordship elegantly expresses himself, may not have been so entirely deprived of tragic pathos, as to offend the taste of the Athenians, whose monuments of art sufficiently shew us, how well they knew the difference between the beautiful and the ridiculous, and how little they need our indulgence in their appreciation of the dignified and graceful.

[1] "Itaque numeros, geometriam, universamque Musicam, rhythmicam harmonicam, metricam, sive contemplativam, sive per instrumenta vocesque promentem se modis variis, accepit ab Ægyptiis doctoribus."—PHILO, *De Vita Mosis*, lib. I.

multitude of the people. The love for music among the Hebrews was the stronger, as it was sanctioned and com· manded by their legislator, and as it became in days of triumph, of exile and captivity, the sole interpreter of the emotions and sentiments of this, at all times, enthusiastic people. In Greece, music was one of the elements of the education of the young ; but their music appeared in the wider acceptation of the word, as mental cultivation through poetry and music. When speaking of applying music to education, we mean nothing else. Poetry is indispensable to vocal music ; and it is vocal music only we think indispensable in education. Lycurgus, following the example of Minos, king of Crete, inspired the Spartans through music to heroism, and taught them to sing, and thus to cherish the laws of the state. " It is certain that the close union of music with the culture of respect for the laws, contributed a great deal to raise music to that high rank which it afterwards occupied in education."[1]

Music and poetry seemed a trifling art at first to Solon, an object of play and amusement only ; but he learned from the Egyptians, that upon the golden wings of these sister arts, every great thought, every philosophical sentence,[2] can be carried into the heart and memory of the singer, and all those who stand listening about him. From that time until his death, the great lawgiver of Athens devoted himself to

---

[1] Wachsmuth's *Hellenische Alterthumskunde*, I. p. 450, and II. p. 374.

Lycurgus, when he came to Crete, engaged Thales to put the laws he destined to Sparta into verse, and to compose the music. Strabo, lib. x. Comp. Plutarch, *Life of Lycurgus*.

Τοὺς Λακεδαιμονίων νόμους ἐμελοποίησε Τέρπανδρος. Clemens Alex. *Strom.* I. 308.

" D'après tous les témoignages (des anciens) on peut donc assurer, que les Lacédémoniens durent presque toutes leurs vertus civiles et militaires aux effets de ce goût pour la musique dont Lycurgue leur avait fait un besoin."—Villoteau, *De l'Analogie de la Musique avec le Language*, vol. II. p. 263.

[2] Τῇ δὲ ποιήσει κατ' ἀρχὰς μὲν εἰς οὐδὲν ἄξιον σπουδῆς, ἀλλὰ παίζων, ὡς ἔοικε, προσχρήσασθαι καὶ περίαγων ἑαυτὸν ἐν τῷ σχολάζειν· ὕστερον δὲ καὶ γνώμας ἐνέτεινε φιλοσόφους, &c. Plutarchus, *Life of Solon*, 3., p. 80.

poetry; composed in verse the *different ages of man*,[1] *his laws, his philosophical works,* the history of the Atlantides, and a great number of elegies.[2] Music, in its wider acceptation, contained the lessons of obedience to the state and its laws; it inflamed to heroism; it taught order, (εὐκοσμία,) in manners, in walk and appearance, moderation, temperance, and veneration of old age, religion; and in general, (the ἀρετή,) every virtue of a good citizen.[3] Out of the poetical genius of the Greek nation, arose the genius of their philosophy. At first, it was not separated from poetry, but we soon see the development of ideas regarding the theogony and cosmogony, the origin and the final destiny of man, give rise to different schools, which, each following its own way, ended, one after another, in the Ionic, the Pythagorean, the Eleatic, the Atomistic and Socratic, the Stoic and Epicurean Schools.

Most of these have treated of music extensively, and given it a place in the education of youth. Their principles in this respect are far from being superannuated, and deserve once more to become an object of serious thought. Before truth and wisdom, before the spiritually beautiful, of which art is the earthly representative, Pythagoras, Socrates, Plato, and Aristotle, equally bowed their head, in thought, reverence, and humility; for, in the beautiful is truth, and the really

---

[1] Clemens of Alexandria has preserved this little work to us in book VI. *Strom.* Compare Philo the Jew on the *Creation of the World.*

[2] Plutarch, *Life of Solon*, p. 106; and Diogen. Laert. *De Vitis Philosophorum*, lib. I.

Luther followed the footsteps of Solon: he not only translated the ancient Latin hymns, but wrote his Catechism and the Confession of Augsburg into verse, in order to have them sung by the people. Henry of Göttingen set even the former into four parts.

[3] Wachsmuth, ib. vol. II. p. 375.

Beautifully has this been expressed by Barthelémy, *On the Music of Ancient Greece:* "Au lieu de s'amuser à rémuer nos petites passions, elle (la Musique Grecque) va réveiller jusqu'au fond de nos coeurs les sentiments les plus honorables à l'homme, les plus utiles à la Société, le courage, la reconnaissance, le devouement à la patrie; c'est que de son heureux assortiment avec la poésie, elle reçoit un caractère imposant de grandeur et de noblesse."—*Voyage du jeune Anacharsis en Grèce.*

true and really beautiful is virtue.[1] Out of the darkness of
human inquiries after knowledge and wisdom, they sought
the inspirations and sublime pleasures which music and poetry
offered them. They themselves were either poets or musicians, or listened with delight to the poetical and musical
effusions of others. Their appreciation and their cultivation
of music has a higher signification to us, as the great object
of their inquiries was man, his natural propensities, his
mental and moral faculties, his will, and his final destiny.
Through them music received its philosophic stamp, its dignity, as a means of contributing to thought and strife, to life
and futurity.

Pythagoras's whole system of education and philosophy was
intimately interwoven with music.[2] Nobility of sentiment
and religious feelings should flow harmoniously, through musical and poetical inspirations, into the soul, and stimulate to
noble actions and pursuits. He knew the power of music in
all its branches, studied its natural laws, and practised it,
with wonderful effect, as art, now to stimulate, and then to
calm the spirits, and thus to harmonize all the human faculties, and to subordinate to the better will every passionate
excitement.[3] His deeper knowledge and more profound acquirements in the art and science of music, command the

---

[1] So much, among the Greeks, was the idea of beauty blended with
moral excellence, that they scarcely separated the one from the other :
καλός, therefore, signifies the physically as well as morally beautiful ;
and καλός ἄνηρ, we would, in the most cases, be obliged to translate,
with a noble, a virtuous, or an excellent man. It is quite in the Grecian
spirit that the German speaks : " Von einer *schönen* Handlung, einer
schönen Seele."

[2] Ἡγούμενος πρώτην εἶναι τοῖς ἀνθρώποις τὴν δι' αἰσθήσεως προ-
φερομένην ἐπιμέλειαν, εἴ τις καλὰ μὲν ὀρώη καὶ σχήματα καὶ εἴδη,
καλῶν δὲ ἀκούοι ῥυθμῶν καὶ μελῶν, τὴν διὰ μουσικῆς παίδευσιν
πρώτην κατεστήσατο, διά τε μελῶν τινῶν καὶ ῥυθμῶν, &c.—Iambl.
V. P. I. c. 15.

[3] Pythagoreis moris fuit, et cum evigilassent, animos ad lyram exci-
tare, quo essent ad agendum erectiores ; et quum somnum peterent, ad
eandem prius lenire mentes, ut si quid fuisset turbidiorum cogitationum,
componerent.—Quintil. *Institut.* IX. c. 4.

Pythagorici, cum diurnas in somno resolverent curas, quibusdam more respect, as he placed music in education in the first rank, and subordinated to it even what they called γραμματική. Thus music was an essential part of study to the Pythagoreans. Our soul, according to them, consisted of harmony, and from what could affect the senses, they hoped to renew the intellectual and primitive harmony of the faculties, which men had lost.[1]

Socrates lamented all his life that he had neglected music in his youth; he applied himself to it in his old age, and replied to the inquiries of the curious with Solon's words: "It is better to learn such an art in old age than never."[2] The day before his death, an Athenian musician sung to him a poem of Stesichorus, accompanied by the lyre: Socrates was so charmed, that he prayed the singer to repeat it until he had learned it. The young man, surprised, asked of what use it would be to him, as he had to die so soon: the sublime answer of Socrates was, "That I may leave this life richer in knowledge."[3] Here we find one of the greatest sages of antiquity, in the face of death, filled with the highest thoughts on the immortality of the soul, taking music for the solace of his last earthly hours, and making of it his companion to the gates of eternity.[4]

To Plato, music was a sacred art; she was the link which tied man, in his earthly exile, to his primitive celestial home, and as a pure companion of virtue, should captivate our heart for all that is good and beautiful. The moral education,

cantilenis utebantur, ut eis lenis et quietus sopor obreperet.—Boethius, *De Musica*, ι. c. 1.

[1] Schiller expresses the same idea beautifully thus: "Man has lost his dignity, but art has saved it : truth still lives in fiction, and from the copy the original will be restored."

[2] Κρεῖττον ὀψιμαθῆ ἢ ἀμαθῆ.—Ammian. *Marcell.* 28, 4.

[3] Ut aliquid sciens amplius e vita discedam.—Ibid.

The same Ammianus tells us a similar fact of Solon, who, as a very old man, wanted to learn an ode of Sappho. He replied to the inquiring musician with almost the same words: ἵνα μαθὼν αὐτὸ ἀποθανῶ: *that I may know it before I die.*

[4] See Beger's *Die Würde der Musik im Griechischen Alterthume*, p. 56. Dresden.

therefore, should begin with music.[1] To nourish the soul with music was of the highest moment; for she penetrates into it, and captivates it with irresistible power. The sense of the beautiful and the good is strengthened, and the dislike of what is common or bad will be deeply rooted, even in that age when reason does not yet teach us to like the one, or to fly the other.[2] With the principles of Socrates, he united a predilection for the laws and institutions of Egypt, and thought that, music being so powerful an agent on the mind, all songs for youth and the people at large, should be examined and approved by law, and that, if music were left to its fate, effeminating songs, and songs destructive to the morals, might become general, and by enervating the noble faculties of man, endanger the state:[3] for, want of order and want of taste in music, is the sister of bad thought, bad language, and habits;[4] and, on the contrary, earnestness and dignity in music, are nearly allied with noble sentiments.[5] In his *Protagoras*, where he speaks of education, he says: " That boys should learn the songs of the best poets, that their souls might become familiar with rhythm and harmony, in order that they themselves might become milder, their mode of life better regulated, so that, both in word and deed, they should acquire earnestness, energy, and consistency; for the whole life of man requires order and harmony."[6] He strove unceasingly to combat the opinion of those who would see

---

[1] Παιδείαν εἶναι πρώτην διὰ Μουσῶν τε καὶ 'Απόλλωνος.—*De Legg.* II. 2.

[2] Ib. II. 1.

[3] Οὐδαμοῦ γὰρ κινοῦνται μουσικῆς τρόποι ἄνευ πολιτικῶν νόμων τῶν μεγίστων.—*De Rep.* IV. 424. c.

[4] 'Αρρυθμία καὶ ἀναρμοστία κακολογίας καὶ κακοηθείας ἀδελφά.—*Ibid.* III. 401. a.

[5] Σώφρονός τε καὶ ἀγαθοῦ ἤθους ἀδελφά τε καὶ μιμήματα.—*Ibid.*

[6] Πᾶς γὰρ ὁ βίος τοῦ ἀνθρώπου εὐρυθμίας τε καὶ εὐαρμοστίας δεῖται.—*Protagor.* 326, 8. Comp. Πᾶσα ἡλικία καὶ σύμπας βίος ἄπασα δὲ πρᾶξις μουσικῇ μόνῃ τελέως ἂν κατακοσμηθείη.—Arist. Quintil. *De Musica,* I. p. 2.

nothing in music but a means of recreation and pleasure. In the second book of his laws, he says: "Most persons say, that the only purpose of music is to give pleasure, but this is a profane, an unholy language: To look on music as a mere amusement, cannot be justified. Music which has no other aim, must neither be considered of value, nor worthy of reverence." Plato's views of art and music have been generally accepted by all superior intellects, although many sages and writers of antiquity have reduced to a greater reality the ideal of the Platonic opinions.

Such also was Aristotle. He who, in all things, especially in political principles, opposed Plato, agreed with him entirely in regard to music. According to him, music should not only be studied for the sake of its power on the morals and manners of a people, but even for the sake of its cheering and recreative influences.[1] It should be considered a part of the education of youth, because it accomplishes two objects—the attainment of the end for which we live, and the recreation on the road to this end. He went farther still, and said, that it was not enough to listen to music only to feel all its advantages, but that it was necessary to practise it. Real enjoyment supposed true understanding, which could only be obtained by practical study.[2]

With the decay of the liberty of Greece, habits and manners degenerated, and with them the fine arts. In the chains of the conqueror, in the servitude of foreign princes, the noble Greek fell into the servitude of the senses. He who, in the days of the glory of his country, had thought, and had combated, sought now nothing more than pleasure and debauchery. Music then became, what it is often now, the companion of revelry. Hence the dislike or the disappreciation of some of the philosophers, who, in their stern virtue, combated against the stream of passion and corruption; hence their condemnation even of music. The cynics, the sceptics, and stoics, were so rough, so exclusive and intolerant in their principles, that, in their eyes, nothing had worth, neither the beautiful in nature nor the beautiful in

---

[1] See 3d and 4th chap. of *Arist. Pol.*   [2] See Appendix I.

art, but virtue alone. Pure joy, according to former philosophers, a child of heaven, was, under Diogenes and Antisthenes, banished as effeminating. Effeminating, especially, was that enjoyment which is the effect of art. Every tender and delicate feeling for humanity, every consideration of mental or bodily suffering, was, to them, effeminacy and weakness. Zeno, harsh, cold, and rough in life as in principles, did, however, not disdain, like many modern puritans, to abandon himself to amusements of a grosser kind, and drank more wine than his morals allowed him to take.[1] In such moments, when his eye was sparkling, and his whole face beaming with delight, the uncouth and rougher nature of the bear would soften, and become even sweet and amiable (ἡδὺς ἐγίνετο καὶ μείλιχος.)[2] They understood the coarser, but not the more delicate part of the nature of man. Nature was their highest principle. Life, thought, and action, should be according to nature, πάντα κατὰ φύσιν; but they understood it in the sense of *naturalia non sunt turpia*, and not in that more noble acceptation of Juvenal, *non aliud natura, aliud sapientia dicit*. Such principles must have made their school, the dirty school, and their persons, outcasts of society, and a real fright to all the five senses.

The opinion of the Epicureans, who made music only sub-

---

[1] There is a striking resemblance between the school of Zeno and some more modern stoics. Pure pleasures, enjoyments, such as fine arts, such as music give, are to be avoided as effeminating, or as seducing snares of Satan. Man should always be grave, always nearer to a tear than to a smile. During the day, even in business, their soul is keeping sabbath; they are in speech, and in appearance, saints and sages; but in the evening they give to their wife and children the melancholy sight of a slave in delirium; they sing like a cow, and walk like a giddy chicken. They are, with all this, of higher and sounder principles; their morals are not as easily alarmed as those of a Grecian cynic. Their philosophy can bear a drowning once a day, and intoxication shows both the dignity of a man, and to what *quantum* he can carry the noble privilege of his species.

That such grosser natures must be enemies of refined arts, speaks, O Music! thy highest praise!

[2] *Athen. and Diogenes Laert.*, vii., 26.

servient to pleasure, deserves no further attention. The principles of Epicurus, who, upon his Elysian gardens, placed the inscription, that pleasure was the highest good,[1] have been well judged, even by Plutarch, who places at the side of Epicurus, the king, Ateas of Scythia, who swore that he preferred rather to hear his horse neigh, than the music of the celebrated Ismenias.[2]

Sextus Empiricus, at last, goes so far as to wage war against music;[3] and it suffices to prove the depth of his philosophical principles, that he says, Epicurus was to him as high an authority as Plato.

Polybius differently appreciated the moral influence of this art. He says, that music was necessary to soften the character of the Arcadians, who lived in a cold, dull country; and that the inhabitants of Cenethæ, who neglected music altogether, surpassed all other Greeks in cruelty, and in the number of crimes that were there committed.[4] However strange this may sound to our ears, the words of Polybius carry with them great weight. He was himself an Arcadian; his talent, judgment, and virtue, were equally admired; he was not less a great practical statesman than an historian; and for his generosity, disinterestedness, and true patriotism, might well be called one of the last of the Greeks.

The learned Plutarch, who might be considered as a link between the ancient and the new era, who, although he lived in the second century after Christ, belonged, as priest of Apollo, to ancient Greece, has transmitted to posterity many treasures of the history and philosophy of antiquity. Among others, he has left us a Dissertation on Music, in which the history and the laws of this art, its beauty, importance, and sublimity, its former grandeur and subsequent decay, form the principal object. In speaking of the power and the importance of music, he begins with the remarkable words : " The

---

[1] Hospes ! hic bene manebis, hic summum bonum voluptas est.

[2] Ὤμοσεν ἥδιον ἀκούειν τοῦ ἵππου χρεμετίζοντος.

[3] Sext. Emp., *Adversus Musicos*.

[4] Polybius' *Hist.*—We give the whole quotation of this remarkable passage in Appendix II.

greatest deeds of eminent generals contributed only to save
some warriors, a town, or a nation, from danger; but they
made those warriors, those citizens, and inhabitants of a country, neither better nor nobler: arts and sciences alone are
fundamental conditions of a truly happy life, of which not
only a family, a state, or a people, but all humanity, feel the
influence; they deserve, therefore, a truly warm and earnest
acknowledgment before all heroic deeds in war."

After having examined all the different opinions of the
Greek philosophers on this art, he says:—" The Greeks
did, not without reason, feel the utmost desire to instruct
the young in music, to form, by its means, their mind and
moral feelings; for music lent assistance to every serious
action, and stood at the side of man even in the dangers
of war."[1] The ancient simple music is, as an invention
of the gods,[2] to be kept in holy reverence. " Music is
something so superior, so divine, so great—something so
beautiful and so sublime, that our forefathers were right
in keeping it in high estimation in education."[3] The ancient Greeks had only music for worship and for education.

Amongst the Romans, Cicero and Quintilianus agree that
music is one of the most powerful agents in ennobling mankind. " I agree with Plato," says Cicero, " that nothing
has so much effect on tender minds as music."[4] One can
hardly say how far its power extends, for the indolent can be
stimulated, the excited can be quieted. " Namque et incitat
languentes et languefacit excitatos, et tum remittit animos, tum
contrahit.[5]

---

[1] Τῶν γὰρ νέων τὰς ψυχὰς ᾤοντο δεῖν διὰ μουσικῆς πλάττειν τε καὶ
ῥυθμίζειν ἐπὶ τὸ εὔσχημον · χρησίμης δηλονότι τῆς μουσικῆς ὑπαρ-
χούσης πρὸς πάντα καὶ πᾶσαν ἐσπουδασμένην πρᾶξιν, προηγουμένως
δὲ πρὸς τοὺς πολεμικοὺς κινδύνους.

[2] Σεμνὴ κατὰ πάντα ἡ μουσικὴ θεῶν εὕρημα οὖσα.

[3] Σεμνὴ ἡ ἁρμονία, καὶ θεῖον τι καὶ μέγα.—ἡ ἁρμονία ἐστὶν οὐρανία,
τὴν φύσιν ἔχουσα θείαν, καὶ καλὴν καὶ δαιμονίαν.

[4] De Leg. ii., 15.

[5] Cicero has elsewhere expressed a similar thought in these words:—
" Nihil est tam cognatum mentibus nostris, quam numeri et voces, quibus

We may, therefore, draw towards the conclusion, and say, that as far as our knowledge of the nations of antiquity extends, according to their own records, we find music held in high estimation, honoured and cultivated by the wisest, the greatest, and the best of men, be they called legislators, sages, or prophets. All nations have considered it a divine gift, sublime in the temple, and cheering at the family hearth; of national festivities the brightest ornament, and in solitude the inseparable companion, the faithful friend of man. As its origin was, by all nations, looked upon as divine, so its true abode was with the gods; and when man, passing through the gate of death, had to leave behind him all earthly possessions, music alone followed him into the mansions of the blest, into eternity; its charms were sought in the Elysium and the Walhalla, as well in Odin's Hall as in Mahomet's Paradise. In the creeds of all nations music has been *eternalized*, by the rougher Scandinavian as well as the more refined Greek; and, according to the Christian doctrines, music will be everlasting:—" There shall be heard a great voice of a multitude, as the voice of many waters, as the voice of mighty thunderings, singing, Hallelujah, glory, honour, and power unto the Lord."

et excitamur et lenimur, et languescimus, et ad hilaritatem et ad tristitiam deducimur."—Cic. *Orat.*, iii. 51.

VI.

Art among the Romans.—Music in the Christian Era, especially in the British Islands.

THE British nation has frequently been compared to the Romans, and the British empire to that of the Roman Cæsars. The comparison may hold good in many points, but, fortunately for Great Britain, not in all. For, if from Athens we turn our eye to Rome, Rome even in its brightest days, we find ourselves, in regard to those manifestations which denote the mental and moral superiority of men and nations, as in a desert. Roman philosophy, Roman art, and Roman literature, stand to that of the Greeks, as the statue of the Gladiator, or the Farnese Bull, to those sublime groups of a Laocoon, or a Niobe. " Poetry had no native growth in Rome," says Schlegel ; this might be said of every art where a deeper feeling, a loftier imagination, a more refined taste, more genius, more humanity, were required. " The Greeks were a nation of artists, and the Romans a practical people."[1] This may appear to many a title of their pre-eminence, and prove the truth of the comparison of the British and Roman nations. But beware of the consequence. There is something terrible in a nation of utilitarians. Where every mind is engrossed with material interests—where every action, every acquisition of knowledge, is calculated by its future produce—where high and low, those who possess much, and those who possess nothing, strive with all their energies, and strain every nerve from the first to the last day of the year, and from the first to the last of their life, to ac-

---

[1] Schlegel, *Dramatic Art and Literature ;* See *Roman Theatre.*

quire more and more wealth and power, to displace the one, to outstrip the other—where nothing has value but what can be exchanged for coin, a society in which material interest is the centre of gravity; in that society there is a deeply-rooted cancer at the source of health and life, which, soon or late, will pay the penalty of the violation of the laws of nature, and the total neglect of the nobler faculties of man.[1]

Compare, then, the practical Romans, with the more ideal Greeks; with them, who made a deeper study of man, his good and evil propensities, his higher destiny, the feelings were not altogether disregarded in education. Heart and mind should harmoniously strive towards the same end of perfection. Compare them, and you will find that the Romans, far from excelling in the fine arts, left their cultivation to the Greeks and Etruscans residing at Rome.[2] The arts were to them articles of luxury, introduced as a corrupting element, both betokening and advancing degeneracy. "In the triumphal processions, the fights of the gladiators and of wild beasts, all the magnificence of the world, all the wonders of every clime, were brought before the eye of the spectator, who was glutted with the most violent scenes of blood. On nerves so steeled, what effect could the more refined gradations of tragic pathos produce? rope-dancers and white elephants were preferred to every kind of art. Desirous as were the Romans to become thorough Hellenists, they wanted for it that milder humanity, which is so distinctly traceable in Greek history, poetry, and art, even in the time of Homer. From the most austere virtue, which buried every personal inclination, as Curtius did his life, in the bosom of fatherland, they passed with fearful rapidity to a state of corruption, by avarice and luxury, equally without example. Never in their character did they belie the legend, that their first founder was suckled, not at the breast of a woman, but of a ravenous

---

[1] Powerfully is this subject treated in the celebrated work of Regier *Des Classes dangereuses de la Société.*—See Appendix.

[2] "Artists were not held in high estimation, and the arts never flourish where they are not honoured."—Dr Schmitz's *History of Rome*, p. 256.

she-wolf. They were the tragedians of the world's history, who exhibit many a deep tragedy of kings led in chains, and pining in dungeons ; they were the iron necessity of all other nations ; universal destroyers, for the sake of raising at last, out of the ruins, the mausoleum of their own dignity and freedom, in the midst of the monotonous solitude of an obsequious world. To them it was not given to excite emotion by the tempered accents of mental suffering, and to touch with a light and delicate hand every note of the scale of feeling. Of all their ancient greatness, nothing remained to them but the contempt of pain and death, whenever an extravagant enjoyment of life must finally be exchanged for them."[1]

These are the words of the man, whose acquaintance with ancient and modern art and literature has scarcely been equalled. They express the sentence of posterity upon one of the greatest nations that ever lived, a practical nation, but a cruel, a hard, a corrupted one—a scourge to mankind, a curse to humanity ; and at whose tomb we have neither tears nor sympathy. From them we would have little to learn in art, if a few master spirits, and above all, Horace, as a splendid star, worthy of Greece, Horace, the Roman Alcæus, had not enlivened the darkness of the Roman night. And, with all his splendour, he is but a child of Greece ; his genius had been nourished with the genius of Greece,[2] as Pindar's with that of Corinna.

If we turn from this great Roman cemetery—upon which a few noble monuments of art, an Ovid, a Virgil, and a Lucullus, stand at the side of Horace—to the British islands, another spectacle of a surprising nature will present itself.

We hear it daily repeated, that Great Britain has neither taste nor leisure for music, and that its cultivation must be sought with those who are less occupied, and have nothing better to do. In a time when almost all Europe is cultivating this art, and begins to associate it with life, when all continental states extend its influence, and give it an impor-

[1] Schlegel, ibid., p. 209.
[2] Princeps Æolium carmen in Italos,
     Deduxisse modos.—*Hor. Od.* iii. 30.

tant share in the education of the young, we find it in the British islands, but mainly in the north of Great Britain, utterly neglected in school and church and families, burdened, persecuted with national prejudices, and in a state of infancy, with regard to its theory and practice, its history and philosophy, unequalled by any other nation. In those times, on the contrary, when all the Occident was still a land unknown to civilization, when wars, and unceasing migrations of northern and Asiatic tribes, kept all Europe in total barbarism, we find music cultivated to such a degree in these isolated islands, that we can say with certainty, that it was never any where more popular, more generally cultivated, or in closer connection with the whole public and private life of a people. The generality of its practice, as our skeleton of facts will shew, seems indeed fabulous, and appears to us, considering its present standing and insignificance, almost like a dream of fairy-land.

Historians have preserved facts concerning the harp of the Celts, which reaches almost to the commencement of the Christian era. Diodorus of Sicily, who wrote in the first half century, says, that the bards sang their poems to instruments like lyres, (ταῖς λύραις ὁμοίων.)[1] The bards stept between the hostile armies with their swords drawn, and their spears extended, and by their eloquence, or by irresistible enchantment, often prevented the effusion of blood. Ammianus Marcellinus (390 of our era) says, that the bards celebrated actions of illustrious men in heroic poems, which they sang to the sweet sound of the lyre.[2]

Skill on this instrument constituted a part of the usual acquirements of the educated class among the Celts as well as the Danes and Anglo-Saxons: in the sixth century, one-third of the male population of Ireland were harpers.[3]

At the convivial repasts of the Anglo-Saxons, the harp passed from hand to hand through all the company. The Saxon poet, Cædmon, in the 7th century, not being able to

---

[1] Lib. v., c. 31, p. 314. Edit. Bipont. [2] Lib. xv., c. 9, p. 89.
[3] Walker's *Irish Bards*, p. 53.

play on such occasions, used to retreat, in order to conceal his ignorance of an art so generally practised among his countrymen.[1]

Bards were considered sacred in their person and property, and their houses were sanctuaries; a harp was considered an indispensable possession, of which a family, in legal pursuits, could not be deprived.[2] The veneration which surrounded the bard, and all that belonged to him, gave him the privilege to pass and repass, in safety, between hostile armies. Thus king Alfred sang (878,) as harper in the Danish camp; and sixty years later, Anlaf, the Danish king, in that of Athelslane.[3]

Adamnan, the Abbot of Iona (700,) says, that singing with accompaniment had been the custom in Ireland among the profane poets or bards, from *remote* and *unknown* time.[4]

In the life of Dunstan, the biographer, a contemporary of the saint (X. Cent.,) says, that the holy man took with him, on his journeys, according to custom, the cythara, called harp in the mother tongue.[5]

The Christian church of the Culdees, of which Bangor in Wales, Banchor in Ireland, and Iona in the Western Islands, were the principal establishments, in many points at variance with Rome, had its own ritual, liturgy, and chant. About that early period (IV. Cent.,) when St. Ambrose endowed the occidental church with his tunes of sublime inspiration, the Culdees had their own tunes; and, according to the specimens preserved to us, not less sublime, and in no degree

---

[1] Beda, *Historia Ecclesiastica*, lib. iv., c. 24.

[2] " The ancient Britons lived and breathed in poetry ; in their political maxims, preserved to our times, they place the poet-musician beside the agriculturist and the artist, as one of the three pillars of social existence." —Thierry's *History of the Norman Conquest*, l. i., p. 53.

See *Trioedd.* beirdd ynys Prydyn, sec. xxi., No. 1. Archaiology of Wales, iii., 283.

[3] See Yugulphus and William of Malmesbury.

[4] Cantum cum modulatione in usum fuisse inter poetas profanos seu Bardos, idque *more antiquo, ab immemorabili.*—Adamnam.

[5] Sumpsit secum Cytharam, quam, paterna lingua, harpam vocamus.

inferior to those of Rome.[1] We learn from Venerable Bede[2] and Bishop Stillingfleet,[3] that the contest between the Roman and British churches commenced with their respective chants. The singers were sent from Rome, monks well skilled in the art: they eventually gained the hearts of those who listened to them ; and thus the Roman chant prepared the way for Roman worship and Roman power.[4] Throughout the middle ages the harp continued to be popular in Ireland. Irish harpers and Irish harps were titles of excellence over all Europe. When Gruffudd ab Cynan, (circa 1100,) a Welsh prince, produced a new code of musical regulations for his Cambrian subjects, a number of Irish bards were invited to Wales, to give their assistance, which was acknowledged with obligation on the part of Caradoc, the historian.[5] In the works of that patriotic and learned Bishop of St David's, Gerald, the Cambrian, who, during his opposition to Henry II., had travelled in Ireland, France, and Italy, we read that Ireland stood, in regard to skill on musical instruments, without comparison, first among the nations he had seen.[6]

Galileo, the father of the astronomer, who devoted almost

---

[1] See Muratori's *Anecdota,* de Antiphonario vetustissimo Monasterii Benchorensis in Hibernia, tom. iv., 121.

In antiquissimo antiphonario *Benchorensi* habes hymnum quando communicarent Sacerdotes : *Sancti venite, Christi corpus sumite.*—Abbas Gerbertus *De Cantu et Musica Sacra,* tom. i. p. 459.

[2] *Historia Ecclesiastica,* lib. iv. c. 18 ; and Vita Abbat. Weremoth.

[3] *Origines Britannicae.*

[4] B. Biscop Psallendi ordinem *juxta Romanum* introduisse in patriam suam Nordanhymbriam.—Beda, *Hist. Abbat. Weremoth,* p. 195., anno 678 ; and *Eccles. Hist.,* iv., 18.

De omnibus ejusdem provinciæ monasteriis ad eundem (archicantorem Johannem,) qui cantandi periti erant, confluebant.—*Ibid.*

We know from Æddius, that he was the first, after the Culdees had been driven away (Scottis ejectis), who instituted the Ecclesiastical Roman Chant (qui cantus ecclesiasticos antiphonatim instituerit) in the monasteries of Northumberland.—Mabillon. *Annal.,* t. i., p. 414 and 494.

[5] Powell's *History of Wales,* pp. 115, 191.

[6] In musicis instrumentis, prae omni natione quam vidimus, incomparabiliter est instructa (gens Hibernia).—*Topog. Hib.,* c. ii., p. 739.

a whole life to the study and inquiry of ancient music, says, in speaking of the harp in Italy: " This very ancient instrument was brought to us from Ireland, as Dante has recorded, where they are excellently made, and in great numbers, and the inhabitants of which island have practised on it for very many centuries."[1]

The harp was such a constant companion of persons of rank, that no one was allowed to be ignorant of it; and no bishop, no abbot, no priest, travelled without the harp ; "for in playing on it, they found, in their piety, great delight."[2]

Also, in Wales, harps were to be found in every family; and the same writer, in describing the primitive manners of the Welsh, and their hospitality to strangers, says, that, " Those who arrive at an early hour are entertained with the conversation of young women, and the music of the harp, till evening ; for here every family has its harps provided for this very purpose. Every family, too, is here well skilled in the knowledge of that instrument." [3]

Remarkable is his passage on the music of Scotland. Those who only know Scotland of the nineteenth century, would not believe in that almost fabulous cultivation of music, 700 years ago, had we nót before us historical documents of such weight and importance. High as he places Ireland, " Scotland has not only equalled but far excelled it; so much so, that Scotland is now regarded as the fountain of the art." [4]

The Caledonian bards were in existence so late as the eighteenth century; their last representatives were Rode-

---

[1] *Dialogues on Ancient and Modern Music.* By Galileo. P. 143. Printed in 1582. Also, in Lord Bacon's *Sylva Sylvarum*, a high compliment is paid to the Irish harps.

[2] Episcopi et abates et sancti in Hibernia viri Citharas circumferre, et in eis modulando pie delectari consueverant.—*Geraldus Cambrensis*, l. c.

[3] Geraldus' *Cambr. Cambriae Descriptio*, c. ix.

[4] (Scotia) non tantum *aequiparavit* Hiberniam, verum etiam in musica peritia *longe prævalet et præcellit ;* unde et ibi quasi *fontem artis requirunt. Topographia Hiberniae*, Distinctio III., c. xi., apud Camdeni Anglic Francofurti, 1602.

rick Morison[1] and Murdoch Macdonald, the former at Dun-
vegan Castle, the latter in that of Maclean of Coll. The
bagpipes have usurped the place of the harp; a poor substitute for the nobler instrument and the nobler race of poet
musicians.

The harpers were of the household of kings and princes.[2]
They slept in the bed-chamber of the kings,[3] and ate out of
their plates, and drank out of their cups,[4] and were at all
times admitted into the king's presence.[5] So high was the
estimation in which they were held, so superior their skill,[6]
so many their privileges, so great the honours bestowed on
them, that, on the one hand, they grew arrogant, exacting,
and overbearing; and, on the other, vagabonds, idlers, and
rogues, assumed their dress and appearance, in order to enjoy their privileges and distinctions. Laws, therefore, were
found necessary to repress the arrogance of the harpers, and
also to protect their dignity and respectability from encroach-
ments of idle adventurers. Acts were passed to prevent their
asking for the king's buckle which fastened his cloak,[7] or for

[1] *Essay on the Highland Music,* by Macdonald, p. 11.

[2] In Domesday Book, the king's minstrel had lands assigned to him as
stated officer. See also, Dr. Percy, v. 1., Introd. p. 64.

[3] Buchanan's *History of Scotland.* See Ethodius 25th, and Fethalna-
chus 38th, king of Scotland.

[4] Froissart tells this of the four Irish kings, who had submitted to
Richard II. at the end of the fourteenth century, and were put under the
care of Henry Castide, to be taught English manners. They refused to
submit to them, and *would not be deprived of their good old customs.*

[5] See interesting anecdote in Walsingham's *History of England.*

[6] Those who are inclined to depreciate, in consequence of the popu-
larity of the harp, the skill required for playing it, have perhaps never
seen or heard the performance of a good Welsh harper. There are still
some rare blind harpers to be heard, who are able, to the amazement of
every musician, to handle the triple-stringed harp (three rows of strings)
in diatonic and chromatic compositions, with a talent, and in a style, with
which modern harpists, with all the improvements in pedals, can only
with difficulty compete. The power of performance, together with the
counterpointed style, in which some Welsh harpers excel, have given us,
of harp and harp-music, and of the bards, in Wales at least, a higher idea
than any we could have formed before.

[7] See Walker's *Irish Bards,* p. 53.

the prince's horse, hawk, or greyhound.[1] That the dignity
of the harper must have been very enviable, as it was capable of satisfying the most exorbitant ambition, has been
proved in many instances. John of Salisbury treats the great
people of his time as following Nero in their extravagances
in behalf of the gold and silver dresses, and embroidered
garments of the minstrels.[2]

The number of those who wished to pass for harpers and
minstrels grew, by degrees, to an enormous amount. Every
mountebank, every tale-teller, every beggar, those who danced,
or played tricks of buffoonery and legerdemain, wore the
cap and cloak of the minstrel, and as such lived upon public
hospitality. That privileged race, therefore, so well received
in every feudal castle, and fondly beloved by the mass of the
people, revered during the barbarous ages and the time of
chivalry, became, by degrees, the terror and plague of the
country. Laws of great severity were passed against " minstrels," " songsters," and " tale-tellers ;" but it would be an
act of injustice to throw the blame upon, and to pronounce
judgment against, the true harpers and minstrels. If we examine the texts of those legal acts with minuteness, we shall
find that they were as much a protection of real minstrelsy
as of the country. That of Edward I. (1315), begins thus :—
" Forasmuch as many idle persons, *under colour of minstrelsy*
 . . . . have ben, and yet be, receaved to meate and
drynke, and be not therewith contented yf they be not largely
considered with gyftes," &c. The law, therefore, restrains
the number of minstrels to be admitted in the houses of pre-
lates, earls, and barons, to three or four a day, and that none
come to " meaner men," unless desired. Edward IV. (1489),
complains, in a letter, that a number of persons falsely assume the privileges of minstrels.[3] The increased severity
of the law seemed to increase the number of such vagabonds.
In vain should the *ear be cut*, or *burned with a hot iron for a*

---

[1] See Jones' *Welsh Bards*, p. 28.
[2] John of Salisbury, in his *Rigordus*, 1185.
[3] *Percy's Relics.* Introduct., pp. 69, 70.

first offence, and the man be *hanged for a second;* acts followed acts, the one more bloody than the other, yet they were still repeated under James VI. (1579, c. 75),[1] and even more than a century later, this kind of vagabondage existed to a most alarming extent. Fletcher of Saltoun computes, in 1698, the number of such characters who, as a real plague, wandered through the counties of Scotland alone, to more than a hundred thousand.[2]

With the introduction and spread of Christianity, there arose a new instrument of music, the organ, producing indescribable effects ; and, remarkable as it may appear, it seems that the organ was in general use in North and South Britain and Ireland, many years before it found a place in the churches of France and Italy.[3] During the thirteenth century, when Italy was recognized as the most eminent school for the practice of that most sublime of all instruments, Florence was visited by organists from all parts of Europe, to hear and see the famous blind performer, called, in consequence, *Francesco Cièco,* and the equally celebrated *Antonio,* surnamed *Dagl' Organi.* Many English and Scottish monks were among those who went to learn and study, and who brought back, over the sea, the knowledge which they had acquired.[4]

In the reign of Queen Elizabeth, whose time produced a Shakespeare, a Bacon, and a Milton, gave also birth to Tallis, Bird, Bull, and many other composers, whose works are still

---

[1] " All minstrels, not avowed in special service by some of the Lords of Parliament, or great Barons," &c.

[2] Second *Discourse on the Affairs of Scotland,* p. 145.

[3] Vide Busby's *History of Music,* Vol. i., p. 264; and O'Connor, *Rerum Hibernicarum Scriptores Veteres,* Vol. iv. *De Organorum et Psalmodiæ usu in vetustis Hibernorum Ecclesiis.*

[4] We have seen and heard, in our own times, the famous Antonio, of whom it might be observed, that as many persons went from Cadiz, the remotest part of Spain, to Rome, in order to see the historian Livy ; so, many most excellent musicians have come from England, *and the most distant regions of the north,* crossing the sea, Alps, and Appennines, in order to hear the performances of Antonio.—*Christophero Landino, Comment. on Dante.*

sung and admired. England then possessed a school of its
own, a school which could compete with the most renowned
of Europe. Music was then generally understood, and knowledge of this art considered a necessary adjunct of a liberal education. Part singing, especially, was then, as the multitude of
compositions of madrigals and canons shew, daily practised
in families, and as under the Anglo-Saxons, the harp, so singing in parts, was in general use after repasts and banquets.
A curious and remarkable instance of the knowledge of music in those times, has been preserved to us in the following
lines : " Supper being ended, and music-books, *according to
the custom*, being brought to the table, the mistress of the
house presented me with a part, earnestly requesting me to
sing. But when, after many excuses, I protested unfeignedly
that I could not, *every one began to wonder*, yea, *some whis-
pered to others, demanding how I was brought up.*" [1]

What was the position of music in Scotland at that time,
we may learn from many historical facts, which, as clearly
as Morley's Dialogue, explain and characterize the whole
period. The extent to which the inhabitants of Edinburgh
practised singing and instrumental music, is to be found in a
most curious and interesting incident which occurred on the
arrival of Queen Mary from France, when many of the inhabitants, to the number of *five* or *six hundred*, attended during
several nights, under the windows of the Abbaye of Isle-
bourgh,[2] (Holyrood,) where the Queen was then staying,
and played on the violins or *rebecs*, and sang psalm tunes.[3]
Whatever may have been the character of the performances,
the above fact fully shews, that Edinburgh had then as many
violins and violinists as perhaps now all Scotland. Music

---

[1] Morley's *Treatise on Practical Musick*.
Thomas Morley, Gentleman of Queen Elizabeth's Chapel, one of the
most celebrated masters in composition,—died 1604.

[2] Edinburgh was frequently so named by French writers of that period.

[3] Brantôme, who accompanied the Queen, says in the *Dames Illustres :*
" Ils lui donnèrent une aubade de mechants violons, et de petits rebecs, dont
il n'y en a pas faute dans ce pays là." John Knox, however, is more
favourable in his account of the performance : he remarks in speaking of

schools existed almost in every town;[1] and remarkable is the statute of King James VI., (issued in the year 1579,) who, as a last and vain effort, tried to save them from utter decay. When we now speak of the organization of music schools, or of music to be added to the daily branches of instruction, we appear to Scotchmen[2] as if we were speaking in a dream. In times so utterly industrial, it passes the limits of the understanding, when there is question of the cultivation and diffusion of an art. However, it is a comfort to say, that it was not always so, as King James's statute most evidently shows: "For the instruction of the youth in the art of music and singing, quhilk is almaist decayit, and sall shortly decay, without tymous remeid be providit, our sovereign lord, &c. . . . requestis the Provest &c. . . . to erect and sett up ane sang scuill, with ane maister sufficient and able for instruction of the youth in the said science of music, as they will answer to his hienes upoun the parrell of their fundationis."

That at that time still considerable skill in music and part singing existed, show us, as well the collections of psalms which were then published in Scotland,[3] as those occasional appearances of the people, who in the streets sang, *two thousand persons in number*, psalms in four parts, at the sound of the Queen : " The melodie lyked hir weill, and she willed the same to be continued sum nychts after with grit diligence."

[1] There were music schools in Ayr, Irvine, Paisley, Glasgow, Cupar, Dunbar, Lanark, Aberdeen, Dundee, Elgin, and St Andrews.—Vide in James Melville's *Autobiography*, concerning his musical studies at St Andrews.

[2] Especially to the Town-Council of Edinburgh.

[3] The psalm tunes published shortly after the Reformation, are in four and five parts, and in *seven* different cliffs, five of which would be now unintelligible hieroglyphics to the greater number of the amateurs and musicians of Scotland. The parts are besides printed, two on one page, and two, but inverted, on the other. This manner of printing is an evident testimony that reading in parts was a common practice in families and churches, where two and two were sitting opposite each other on a table or in a pew, and read from the same book. Compare " *the Psalmes of David in Prose and Meeter, with their whole tunes in foure and more parts, with same Psalmes in Reports.* Printed at Edinburgh by the heires of Andrew Hart, *Anno Dom.* 1635."

which, as the historian says, *heaven and earth resoundit, and singer and listener were moved to tears*.[1]

We close here the series of documents concerning the high cultivation of music in the British Islands. We have met with incontestable facts, proving that music has as favourable a soil in Great Britain and Ireland, as elsewhere. Without the annals of past centuries, however, such an assertion would find an unbelieving ear. The present state of this neglected art (in Scotland at least,) is so destitute, that without the faith in the universality of music, and without a glance into the history of past ages, it would be too great a stretch of imagination, to believe that music ever was a popular art, far less to such a fabulous extent; for out of hearing of the concert-rooms and theatres, we stand, in regard to music, in a land of exile; we tread the ground of a cemetery. We ask in vain for the schools, the choirs, the works and masters of former days. A misunderstood piety has carried them to the grave. A gift that providence found worthy of giving to man, should have been found worthy of preserving: but it is not so. Silence surrounds us on every side; the children are silent in the schools; silent is the united multitude in churches, or if they raise their voices and mean to sing, it is in a style, compared with which the singing of a Moravian congregation of the Hottentots would appear as a choir of angels. The teacher of the people in the church, and the teacher of the people in the school, have not felt the absence of this heavenly art of sound within their walls. Instead of seeking it above their horizon, as a sublime power to open the heart and the understanding, they seek it in the lower regions, and look down upon it, from their imaginary throne of superiority, as upon a lovely woman, both the mother and the victim of debauchery and seduction.

Yes, it is far in space and time, from the shriek of the engine-whistle to the simple and sublime chants, the sacred

---

[1] Calderwood the historian has furnished us with the most minute description of this incident, which happened at the return of Durie, one of the town ministers, from exile.—See also the *Letters and Journals of Robert Bailie*, edited by David Laing, vol. III.

musical inspirations of the fathers of the church; it is far away from the Forth and the Tweed to that dwelling in Wittenberg, where a Mathesius, a Melancthon, and a Luther passed half nights in singing mottets, and the *dulces exuviae*, the last words of Virgil's *Dido*.[1] It is a long time from our days to those of Zuinglius, who could sing and play,[2] and nevertheless, could speak as a Demosthenes, and die upon the field of battle.

If history tells us that music may be a luxuriant plant of the British soil, these men teach us that music is also a religious art; that it is a sacred legacy of the fathers and founders of Christianity, and of the founders and martyrs of the Reformation; a legacy, which in the hands of those who should be its guardian priests, instead of being watched and guided, cultivated with zeal, with care and jealousy, has been allowed to sink deeper and deeper, more and more neglected in church and school, and more and more deprived of all its sacred attributes. How well would the words of Zuinglius be applied to his misled, his degenerated followers! " If thou knewest what music is, the evil spirit of ambition, power, and controversy, the demon of riches, luxury, and avarice, would instantly be driven out of thee."

What a terrible sentence must, to their ear, appear the words of the energetic and learned author of the Reformation, when he says : " I do not think that through the scriptures all fine arts should be condemned, as many would-be theologians·do : I want to see the arts, especially that of music, in

---

[1] Mathesius, (*Historien von Luthers Leben*, Bl. 155,) who was frequently a guest on these occasions, says, " We often sang the last words of Virgil's *Dido*. Master Philippus (Melancthon) also sang with us."

[2] Vide Bullinger. In the MS. preserved at Zurich, this writer says of Zuinglius, " That although his adversaries called him the Evangelical Piper, he continued to cultivate music with great modestie ;" and when Faber (afterwards Bishop of Vienne) reproached him for his cultivation of music, he said, in his noble simplicity : " Tu ne sais pas, mon cher Faber, ce que c'est que la musique : J'ai, il est vrai, appris à jouer du luth, du violin, et d'autres instruments : Ah, si tu connoissais le son du luth celeste, l'esprit malin de l'ambition et de l'amour des richesses qui te possèdent sortiraient ainsi de toi."

the service of him who has given and created it."[1] Therefore he mentions : " Children must learn to sing, and teachers
must be able to teach it.   Music stands nearest to divinity !
. . . I would not give the little I know, for all the treasures
of the world ! She is my shield in combat and adversity, my
friend and companion in moments of joy, my comforter and
refuge in those of despondency and solitude."

[1] Preface to his *Geistlichen Liedern.*   Wittenberg, 1544.

VII.

The Present System of Musical Education—Musical Teaching in Boarding
Schools—The Different Styles of Composition.

MUSIC then, as we have shown, stands in connection with
education, with classical and popular education ; and the
objection that its cultivation has no native soil in the British
Islands, is proved to be unfounded. That it is also a part of
religious training, has in a few words sufficiently been expressed. But all obstacles, all prejudices, are not therefore
removed, and at every step new ones arise and obstruct our
path. We hear many teachers and directors of educational
institutions say, that already a great deal of time and attention on their part, and too great a share indeed on the part
of the parents, was already given to music, and that the time
its study requires, was altogether out of proportion with
other branches of instruction ; and that, after all, they could
not see in what consisted the superiority of those who had
acquired superiority in music ; and that even many musicians
were far from being an ornament to society, and luminaries
in the moral world ; that, on the contrary, they seemed even
to have been more prodigally provided with human weakness
than the rest of mankind, and that their thirst for knowledge
and wisdom, revealed itself only in their unquenchable thirst
for all good things of this earth.—These objections are serious ; they place music before a high tribunal. Here it stands
before the bar of an implacable judge—experience—before
whose terrible sentence even the authority of a Plato and a
Luther must remain mute and of no avail. This is a language which is not uncommon, and which, applied to a considerable portion of the craft, is unfortunately too true. As

a great share of the still existing fears for a musical education, especially for young men, is attributed, and rightly so,
to the social meetings to which music might lead, and to that
dense atmosphere in which a number of musicians are known
to live and exhibit their skill and talent, it is necessary, before speaking of general musical education, to say a few
words on the education of those whose principal and exclusive study and profession it is.

The abuse which professional men make of the art, has
its source in a too superficial, too partial, too one-sided development of their faculties. The mind and the heart, as
said before, should be developed simultaneously, and receive
nourishment from the cultivation of the understanding and
of the sentiments. Nothing is so baneful in its consequences
as the unfolding of one faculty to the prejudice of the others ;
the connection between the different branches of human
learning is too intimate, too delicate, to admit of the attention being devoted exclusively to one alone. The ignorance
of musicians has been often remarked. J. J. Rousseau said
a great deal in these few words : " *les musiciens lisent peu ;*"
their inebriety also is proverbial, and has acquired for them
a lamentable celebrity. These facts bear a date of long
standing, for, besides the very ancient proverb of the church,
cantores amant humores, translated in French by *Ivrogne
comme un musicien*, Titus Livius tells us, that when the
censors forbade the flautists to eat and drink in the temples, they quitted the city of Rome, and went to dwell at
Tibur. There being then no musicians for the religious
service, the senators were much embarrassed. But the Ti-
burians came to their aid. The decided passion of the Tibi-
cinists for drink was known : their hosts invited them to a
great feast. Their throats, dried up by the flute, were frequently moistened by wine, until at last, by dint of continued
libations, every one of them, without exception, fell dead
drunk ; in this state they were transported back to Rome,
and were not a little surprised when they awoke on the
forum, under the shouts of the populace. The Senate then
laid hands on them, but, instead of punishment, they were

henceforth allowed to continue eating and drinking, for it seems that nothing short of this could set the flutes again agoing. This miserable failing, so derogatory to the noble profession of musician, and which probably has produced the Latin diction, *musice vivere, musice ætatem agere*, for a life of debauchery, is perpetuated in many of its followers; for we learn that under Louis XIV. the principal band of musicians received on the fête days of St Louis and St Martin, bread and wine to their hearts' content. The minstrels used to partake of the latter to such excess, that they almost always appeared before the king with their eyes starting from their sockets, no longer in condition to play in time; and notwithstanding the conductor's staff, *gavots, minuets*, all would go pell-mell, to the utter despair of the royal auricles. Even the king of the minstrels, in spite of the high dignity with which he was invested, saw neither notes nor musicians, and could distinguish no sharp from a flat. J. J. Rousseau relates of his professor of music, M. Lemaître, what might be still said of many others: " He was as good a drinker as he was a musician; his inspiration augmented in proportion as the liquid in his bottle diminished; and if he were captivated by the charms of composition, he was no less so by those of wine." [1] On proceeding with this original sin of musicians, we may sometimes find it among eminent composers; among those who, while moving in the regions of high tragic poetry, are, in reality, walking, like Robert Macaire, upon the upper leather of their boots. These are not proofs of a high vocation, although they may be found even in men of genius; but they are, to a certainty, proofs of a deficiency of general education, or of the cultivation of one faculty at the expense of all others. A man may be a star in his profession, and there possess great eminence, and yet be, in every other sphere, in infantine ignorance. A great mathematician, a superior chemist, an excellent lawyer or physician, may be a very uneducated man. Education extends over the moral and intellectual faculties, harmonizes all the various

[1] *Confessions de J. J. Rousseau.*

branches of knowledge; and, in this union, it manifests itself
not only in thought and action, but even in language, in
manners, and external bearing.   If, therefore, we find among
a certain lower order of musicians, those propensities which
have caused them so sad a celebrity, and created against music such apprehensions, it is evident that their art stands beyond the reproaches which their intellectual inferiority, their
deficiency of general education, alone deserves.   Every thing
holy may be abused, religion as well as art ; yet they remain
unchanged, though often administered by unworthy hands.

But even this abuse of music, why make it a subject of reproach to music itself, or to musicians, when, on the contrary, musicians should ask you to account for it ?   Does
not Plato, for twenty-two centuries, warn the legislators of
the abuse of music, and recommend to their care its purity ?
Has he not foretold, that unless its sacred character, its
power and importance, were jealously preserved to the youth,
to the nation, to the state, it might be turned, in corrupted
hands, against the youth, against the nation, and against the
state ?   Whence does music receive its greatest injury, its
deepest wounds ?   From those who should be its natural
guardians, the most jealous defenders of its beauty and
purity—the parents of children, and the managers of schools,
especially schools for female education.   To study music is,
to them, nothing but to learn to *play the piano*.   You may
have talent, or you may have none, you must learn it under
penalty of being taxed with having received but an indifferent education.   In what, then, consists this study of the
piano ?   In sitting so many hours *daily* before the instrument, having the fingers curved, and stretched, and trained ;
and after having thus passed, in the most tedious and
thoughtless of all studies, the most precious and invaluable
hours of life, what knowledge has been acquired ?   Have
they become musicians for their pains ?   Has the science of
music been revealed to them ?   Have they learned to understand. to judge, to analyze a musical composition in its technical construction and poetical essence ?   Or, have they
learned to produce, after their own impulse, a musical

thought, to develope it, and, in a momentaneous inspiration, to make the heart speak in joyful or plaintive strains, according to their mood of mind? Nothing of the kind. A few have learned to play a *sonata*, perhaps a *concerto*; a greater number have reached variations, but by far the greatest majority only quadrilles! This playing of quadrilles, this training of the fingers, mothers complacently call *accomplishment*, a *refined education*; and musicians who look with contempt upon musical study and musical works of this description, can they be surprised when the art to which they have devoted themselves, is not appreciated, not understood? What can we expect, when its whole destiny is left in the hands of matrons of boarding-schools, who, generally, are clear-sighted enough to make it an important *item* of their business, withdraw the lion's part from what is due to the teacher, but are ignorant of its very alphabet.[1]

If, in musical education, great errors are committed by teachers, the greatest of all arises from their submitting to the tyranny of these matrons, and their complacency in satisfying the wishes and the vanities of the parents. Unacquainted with music, its loftier purposes, and even with its mechanical department, the latter are over-anxious, in their paternal solicitude, to hear their offspring play or sing great pieces. The day is fixed beforehand, when, at a certain party, the young prodigy should take the whole company by surprise. The teacher, or governess, are alone initiated into the secret; and

---

[1] Every cow in Switzerland knows the bells of her own herd, and distinguishes the air (Rans des vaches) of her herdsman from that of any other; but we know managers of boarding-schools, where the pianoforte tinkling is going on from morning to night, to the great delight of the quarter bills, who flatter themselves that they cannot distinguish Rule Britannia from God Save the Queen. Their musical knowledge seems to extend as far only as that of Dr Johnson, who could distinguish a drum from a trumpet, and a bagpipe from a guitar. Boswell, his biographer, says, that he was very fond of the bagpipe, but instead of admiring it, as other people do, at a certain distance, he put his ear close to the great drone, which was certainly a little beyond what the nerves of an ass might be able to stand, and which would be enough to drive to insanity the most unmusical of all brutes.

these poor martyrs of ignorance try every means to show the
star in all its magnitude. The day, the great day, arrives;
the company begin to gather; the grandpapa has taken his
arm-chair, and now, O misery! begins the musical entertainment. Papa feels quite uneasy; mamma is in a fever; and
the juvenile Corinna is all but fainting. However, the glorious moment has come when the sun is to rise and dazzle
every eye. We all have heard such prodigious performances.
One bar after the other makes slowly its appearance, and is,
as it were, forced out; when she sings, it is in stammering
notes that she produces the eloquent *A te o cara*, or, *Una
furtiva lagrima*. Often overcome with fear and emotion,
not of the music, but of the heads and candles around her,
she stops short, goes on again, but, alas! the black and white
keys begin to melt into each other, and to interchange
colours, until—all is darkness and confusion. So ends the
first musical entertainment, and so begins the musical career
of young persons in general : each party-day is a new disap-
pointment for the family and visitors, and a day of deep distress for the poor victim of such vanities and follies.

It is very certain that music, so acquired, must become
irksome and tedious, that it can offer no enjoyment for the
moment, no nourishment for the mind, and throughout a
whole lifetime, no compensation for the time, the money,
and the tears it has cost. In going directly against the purpose, it would be unreasonable to expect to attain it. We
would wish to learn and love music; but you teach us to
dread and to hate it :—a system which resembles that of the
night police, who carry lanterns, that the thieves may see
them from a distance. Well may we say to those parents,
and boarding-school Minervas, that music is a dangerous art,
if thus it becomes, in their unholy hands, an instrument of
torment to the young, or if it has to pass as a blighting
blast over the happy days of youth, and is, thanks to them,
a handmaid of vanity, an empty, idle, stupid show, on the
one side, and a greedy, cunning speculation, a vile, contemptible trade on the other. Well may we say to the musician,
who thus sacrifices his dignity, betrays the art, and, as a sor-

did usurer, sells it to the highest bidder, what Schiller said
to the literary tradesman: " Unhappy mortal! who, with
science and art, the noblest of all instruments, effectest and
attemptest nothing more than the day-drudge with the
meanest; who, in the domain of perfect freedom, bearest
about thee the spirit of a slave."

" But," continues he, " how is the artist to guard himself
from the corruption of his time? By despising its decisions.
Let him look upwards to his dignity and his mission, not
downwards to his comforts and his wants."

As we do not expect to change this degrading system
of musical education, unless the parents show a better understanding and a higher appreciation of the art, it is to
them we expose the necessity of a total reform in musical
tuition, and say, either release the child entirely from this
odious, mechanical, and stupifying study, good only for
nourishing ostentation and self-conceit, or make it a rational,
intellectual, and noble agent of moral education and mental
refinement. The more solid, the more elementary the beginning, the sooner the end is attained. All those who learn
music with the view to shine, will never learn it to satisfy
the better judge. They will find the general road too long,
and, unlike common mortals, begin where others finish; fly
without wings. They learn, by heart, like a bird, a *Cavatina* and a great *Aria*, and display their science in drawing-
rooms, turning henceforth—a living hurdy-gurdy—in endless rotation, from the Cavatina to the Aria, and from the
Aria to the Cavatina. How different those who have learned
thoroughly the principles of music! they sing every choral
or solo composition, though never seen before.

As soon as we approach music with more earnestness and
intelligence, as soon as we ask for its deeper sense, its worth,
we find that neither a common mechanical study, nor a common acquaintance with some of the inferior musical productions, can suffice. Music has its different spheres in which
it moves, different according to its character and its tendency. In its lowest, it has no other aim than to reach the
ear, to please, to charm it, to amuse for a moment, and

then to pass hence with the same breath of air which brought it. To this sphere belong the greater part of those musical compositions which have as yet reached the generality of amateurs. The endless variations, those numerous songs, duets, and trios, in which a foreign language and exotic melodious form have the great share of attraction, belong to this class. Many songs, glees, and other vocal compositions in the native language, are nòt, in their poetical and musical thought and form, much more deserving of attention. Hours of study spent on such, often worse than senseless combinations of words and sounds, are hours lost in life.

Music has its low and lofty branches ; like architecture, it has its gradations, its huts, its palaces, and cathedrals. The greater part of the playing and singing multitude, have not yet extended their acquaintance beyond the hut and cottage region of the art. Or, if we take painting as our measure of comparison—arias, duets, and trios, vocal or instrumental, however beautiful, belong only to that rank of musical composition, in which stands a *portrait* or *genre* painting, scenes of common life, like Adrian van Ostade's village fairs, groups of dancers, drinkers or fiddlers ; or like Morillo's Savoyards, monks, and beggars. Quartettes, overtures, symphonies, though the latter have, by the genius of Mozart and Beethoven, been placed upon the broadest, the grandest basis, and have risen to an almost unproportioned height, will never reach beyond the standard of the landscape. They stand at the side of those vivid and elegant scenes of a Canaletto, and now speak the touching pastoral language of a Poussin in his Arcadia, or disclose nature, like a Salvator Rosa, in all her grandest, wildest, most terrific moods. Choral and orchestral compositions, in which music and poetry go hand and hand in the development of a lofty, a moral, or sacred idea, ·rank with historical works in painting, with temples and cathedrals in architecture, in glorious supremacy over the humbler divisions of the art. In this region we meet those great spirits who, with their works, have both enlightened and astonished the world ; an Animuccia and a Perugino, a Palestrina, at the side of a Michael

Angelo, an Orlando Lasso, a Philippus de Monte, a Siciliani, a Morales, a Vittoria, vying with a Titian, a Tintoretto, a Correggio. Here we meet those glorious names of an Allegri, a Durante, Lotti, Caldara, the Scarlattis, and Bachs, and Hasse, and Handel, grouped together like the Pleiades of the musical constellation. Compare with such names and works, those which we find in the musical library of our amateurs. You will· see the sphere in which they move : then you will often peruse a number of large volumes, without finding one single composition which would captivate the interest of a real musician ; not one which he would think good enough to be put into the hands of his pupils or children. What sacrifices, what hours, what precious years, are wasted in the acquisition and practice of a kind of composition, which, in reality, belong only to, what we might call, the musical infirmities and excrescences ! Such compositions are the productions of musical merchants, written for the market, and calculated upon the ignorance of the customers. The distance of such a musician to a Palestrina, a Handel, a Mozart, can only be measured by that from an *ignis fatuus* to one of the luminaries of the ether above us. The same space lies between works of their creation ; the one is like an earthen pot fit for common purposes ; the other, the lofty effusion of a lofty mind, sprung from the immeasurable depths of the feelings and emotions of a noble heart, aiming at the beautiful, the great, and the infinite. In them all is spirit, enthusiasm, and poetry. Whoever approaches the sphere in which they breathe, feels himself elevated, and upon the wings of genius, carried away into other zones, other climes, more congenial with the spiritual, the immortal man. There he lives with a Raphael, a Schiller, a Mozart, in the regions of the ideal, and tastes, in those moments of light and purity, joys which the world can neither grant nor take away, which no recollection can either darken or efface. Their works are not temporary in their effect ; they leave traces wherever they pass, indelible remembrances. "*They cease,*" says Zelter, "*but they are not done ; in them there is no end.*"

Should such works of genius exist in vain? Should they remain a dead letter to the most of us? Should a ballad, a glee, a madrigal, close our musical horizon? Is there nothing more beyond this narrow space of atmosphere, in which we turn and return like a water-wheel, without moving one step in advance? Can we remain in this musical infancy? Have we not to rise out of this circle of musical trivialities, and, through a closer acquaintance with its technical and scientific principles, try to approach nearer to the sanctuary of the temple of art, and to be initiated in its loftier inspirations? There are elements enough about us, to raise music from its lowest to its highest station; and soon we might be able to say, in every school, in every institution, with Zelter: "Our chorus is now nothing less than a vast organ, which I can set a-playing or stop with one movement of my hand, and can make it, like a telegraph, denote and express great thoughts;—an organ, every pipe of which is a rational, voluntary agent, and which may realize our highest conception. Our choir is a school, whose end is wisdom, whose means, poetry, harmony, and song."[1]

[1] Zelter's *Briefwechsel mit Göthe.*

VIII.

Vocal Music: its influence upon the Health of Children, and upon the Development of the Physical Organs.

WE have spoken, in the former part of this work, of the nature of the various senses; we have deduced the necessity of the cultivation of the ear from its power, its direct and immediate influence upon the moral faculties, and the intimate connection existing between both; and have now reached the moment when we must shew, in all their special bearing, the influence which the cultivation of vocal music exercises upon the development of our external organs, and indicate the ways by which it unfolds by degrees the internal nature, the moral part of man.[1]

The various parts of the human body, in order that they may be kept in a healthy and active condition, require to be exercised according to the different functions assigned to them by nature. We are provided with a voice having the two-fold power of articulating words, and of uttering musical sounds. We may thence conclude, that both singing and

---

[1] For more particulars, we must refer the reader to the Introductory remarks contained in our Elementary Manuel, *Singing for the Million*, where the subject is treated under the following heads:—

1. *Influence of Singing on Physical Education in general, and on the health of children in particular.*
2. *Influence of Singing upon Moral Education.*
3. *The most suitable Age for Instruction in Singing.*
4. *Singing Exercises and Songs for Children.*
5. *Simultaneous Instruction in Elementary Schools.*
6. *Musical Education in Germany.*

From p. i. to p. xxiii.

speaking contribute to maintain, and even to improve, the healthy state of the various muscles and other organs, called into action when these physical faculties are exercised.

One of the first benefits arising from vocal instruction, is improvement in speaking. It has been justly asserted, that singing is the most effective means of improving the organs, if naturally good, and of correcting them if defective. In the manner of speaking, as well as of singing, as in the voice itself, there is a marked difference in different persons. This difference consists in more or less facility of utterance, more or less agreeableness of pronunciation, and in the peculiar tone with which nature has provided each individual. However various the shades of voice and tone, the practice of singing will be for all, we are sure, a never-failing means of improvement.

Instruction in singing serves to develope and cultivate not less the sense of hearing, the organs of which, like those of the voice, are not equally perfect in every individual. A great error will therefore be committed, in depriving those children of singing lessons who do not, in the first instance, evince a decidedly musical disposition, or what is popularly termed a musical ear. That quality is developed much more slowly in some persons than in others; there are some, indeed, in whom it seems totally deficient; but its absence often proceeds from their seldom or never having heard singing, and from their consequently not having had the opportunity of imitating the tones of others. By listening to singing, we learn to distinguish the relative position of the notes uttered by the voice; our ear thus becomes practised, and able to convey the nicest distinction of tone to the seat of perception. Thus, by endeavouring gradually to imitate others, we succeed in rendering the organs of voice capable of reproducing the sounds which the ear has received.

We come now to consider the influence of singing on the health of children. One of the prejudices most obstinately maintained against teaching children to sing, arises from an opinion frequently broached, that singing, if practised at a tender age, may have a baneful influence on the health, and occasion pulmonary affections. It is not long since this idea prevailed in Germany also; but the most minute investigations, made by governments as well as parents, have proved it to be quite erroneous. From the many thousand instances of contrary results, the German people have at last learnt the utter fallacy of this notion, and have not only ceased to dread singing as being injurious to health, but go so far as to consider it one of the most efficacious means, not only for refining the ear, for developing the voice, but also for giving strength and vigour to all the physical organs it calls into action. Nothing is better calculated than the practice of singing, to produce the power of free and lengthened respiration. In proportion as matter is soft and plastic, it receives impressions the more readily and indelibly. The human body is necessarily subject to this physical law; and its mysterious union with the living principle, and with spirit, must contribute to increase rather than diminish the effect of that law. Childhood is the fittest period to receive to its fullest extent all the advantages resulting from this branch of instruction. All the organs of the voice are then soft and flexible, and susceptible of the slightest impression. The lungs expand with unobstructed ease; the muscles and nerves connected with the throat and chest, yield readily to the action of respiration; the ear receives and conveys sound with facility, and ideas communicated at that early epoch of life are not easily effaced.

On the whole, then, we are convinced that singing, or, as it may be termed, the art of extending and managing breath, is one of the best preventives of, and surest remedies for general weakness of the chest; and that its use, provided always it be proportioned to the other physical powers of the singer, is calculated to exert a most favourable influence on delicate constitutions, to impart vigour to the organs connected with the lungs, and thus to conduce to a healthy state of those important functions of the body.

Those who assert, that children who learned to sing early have lost their voices, do not take into account the thousand accidents and changes to which their constitution, by our effeminate training, may be subjected ; disease of any kind, violent colds, and whatever else may have weakened the chest, and destroyed the former better quality of the voice. At that period of life when the voice undergoes a change, boys lose theirs altogether ; the notes of a higher pitch disappear one after another, till, by degrees, a new one presents itself upon a lower octave of the scale, in the form of a Tenor or a Bass. Often an excellent Treble is, in the space of a few months or a few weeks, replaced by a Bass of the roughest kind. Although the Female voice does not undergo such a remarkable transformation, it nevertheless changes its whole character : a low voice often becomes a high one, and a high one descends and becomes a Contralto ; a good voice changes into an indifferent one, and *vice versa*. This depends entirely upon the development of the bodily frame and the state of health, so that no one can say, with certainty, what the voice of a child will be at a more mature age. The loss of voice is therefore unjustly attributed to *early singing*, unless injudiciously chosen exercises, or too high notes, have occasioned efforts beyond the power of the voice and chest. Besides, every one knows that children, playing in the open air, often exercise their vocal powers more in *one* hour, by violent exclamations, than a judicious teacher would ask them to do in a year.

The earliest age, that of six or seven years, is the most appropriate for learning to sing ; voice and ear, so obedient to external impressions, are rapidly developed and improved, defects corrected, and musical capabilities awakened. Experience of many years, and observation of every day's occurrence, have taught us, that a considerable proportion of the numerous children with whom we have met, could *at first* neither sound a single note, nor distinguish one from another ; ALL, without exception, have acquired ear and voice, and some of them have even become superior in both to their apparently more gifted companions ; in others, the very weak or indifferent voices have in a short time become pleasing, strong, clear, and extended.

Children, from five to six years of age, some of them unacquainted with the letters of the alphabet, have learnt to read music, to a considerable extent, in unison and parts, and to sing, with astonishing precision, imitations and fugues of Hiller, Rink, Fuchs, Teleman, and other great masters. So thoroughly acquainted have they become with the pitch of sound, that, without the least hesitation, they name the notes of which melodious phrases are composed, as soon as sung or played; and it is remarkable, that in this exercise the youngest, and those who had at first to contend with the greatest difficulties, appeared the most acute and ready.

This improvement is more or less rapid. Some children having no ear at first, became awakened to the distinction of sound in a few days, some in a few weeks, and others after months only.

After having seen in a thousand instances, what interest, what intense pleasure children, we might say infants, take in their little singing lessons, after we have seen the astonishing progress they make, we are convinced that, through the medium of such early instruction, musical dispositions may be awakened in a surprising degree. Thus a taste, a true appreciation of this beautiful, innocent, and delightful art, may be created at a very early period, and its charming effects extended over a whole existence.

We have seen children whom their parents believed to be totally devoid of any taste or faculty for music, attend singing classes with the most unexpected success. Their interest in music grew, and with it their knowledge and their voice. With several children, a few weeks practice sufficed to change the entire character of their voices, which, though at first weak and indifferent, and of almost no extent, became strong, extended, clear, and, in some cases, of even a fine quality. Such instances are best calculated to dispel the prejudices existing against musical instruction at an early age.

It would be useless, however, to expect such results from individual tuition. We know by experience, that when children are brought together, they imperceptibly impart cheerfulness, and stimulate each other to exertion and activity; thus, the influence of singing upon the ear and voice, and in the health and morals of the pupils, will be increased tenfold, when aided by the participation of numbers in this pleasurable exercise; the delicate and nervous child will gain strength and confidence, and the slow and indolent be roused. Imitation, that powerful spring of human action—the example of their little companions, their progress, and even their mistakes—furnish the teacher with the means of making his lessons more interesting and successful, than he could ever render them by individual tuition, however great his zeal or talent. And so we find, that the children take that intense interest in their lessons which, at their age, is in general only bestowed on play; at home, the influence of singing extends itself to their habits and dispositions, and consequently to their moral character.

In short, such facts certainly speak in favour of the musical nature of the youth of Great Britain, and we wonder if we shall again have to listen to the old-fashioned prejudice, 'that Music can only grow on German or Italian ground, and that England is not a musical country.' But cannot the senses, which are common to us all, be in England, as well as in Germany, cultivated, refined, and *educated?* for it is education that developes the dormant faculties of nature, awakens the latent spark of genius, and unfolds, in wondrous ways, the secret powers of heart and intellect.

With regard to young persons, comparatively less advantages are to be expected than from children. The nerves and muscles to be exercised in singing have no longer the same elasticity; the voice and ear are less flexible; and the teacher has lost that creative power, which he possessed in so high a degree during the period of infancy. Then he could awaken musical faculties, form an ear, call forth a voice, inspire a love for music, and break through every obstacle. If we consider, besides this, that young persons are overwhelmed with varied studies, and cannot have their thoughts so concentrated upon this branch of instruction, we may say, with certainty, that those who have not learned the elements of vocal music before their 10th or 12th year, have lost the most favourable period of their life—a loss which nothing but zeal and perseverance, and particular musical talent, can redeem. Throughout life, the difference between a musician from infancy, and one from more mature age, will be visible at a glance. The latter may possess musical knowledge and taste ; the former will possess both, with deeper musical feeling, more power, and greater certainty of judgment. In the one, music will be an acquirement; in the other, a feeling, a new sense interwoven with the constitution, a second nature. With children, the teacher has a power of creation ; with adults, he is dependent on circumstances ; he educates in the one case, in the other he has to amend the defects of education. The errors and prejudices in regard to vocal instruction are so great, that in general it is begun only when it should cease, and when the greatest care of the teacher alone can avert fatal consequences. It must, however, be evident to every intelligent mother, that when the voice changes its scale and character, and assumes another for life, it is no time to begin to sing ; on the contrary, this is the time not to sing, or to do it with great care, avoiding every violent exertion ; then a voice may be destroyed, not in infancy, when every trial is gain, every exercise is strength.

Besides the physical difficulties, another, not less prejudicial, presents itself ; and this is, the defective musical education which young ladies have previously received in the tedious and mechanical study of the piano. Instead of learning the poetical part of music and its higher bearings, the pupils in general pass year after year in the drudgery of seeking mechanical perfection, hardly even acquiring the exterior form, and never looking below the surface for a thought or the connexion of ideas. If, in learning music, it is not the object to learn its meaning, to understand and enjoy the deeper sense hidden under the beauty of the form, it is scarcely worth the trouble, and certainly deserves not, as a mere fashion, the sacrifice of so much labour, and so many of the most interesting moments and best years of life.

Singing is the foundation of all musical education, and ought to precede the study of any instrument. In singing classes, children learn to read at sight, and are made acquainted with the

general elements of the art, before their attention is called to
the mechanical part of it. Thus prepared, they appreciate
and enjoy the study of an instrument, instead of finding it,
as is usually the case, tedious and interminable. Years of
pianoforte instruction may be spared in following this more
rational plan, universally recognized and adopted in Germany, with such practical advantage.

In order to remedy, as far as possible, this kind of musical
education, adults will have to begin from the commencement,
and pass, though more rapidly than children, over the elementary parts. Notwithstanding the obstacles which scarcity
of time for practice, and more hardened natural organs, op-
pose, they may still attain a considerable facility in reading
in parts ; the voice may be cultivated, rendered more flexible, and above all, more expressive. The principal object
of the teacher must be to draw the attention to the more
poetical part of music ; to explain the variety of form, the
difference of character and style, and the consequent expression in the performance of solo compositions. Thus he may
still succeed in imparting, as far as practicable, a thorough
knowledge of its theory and practice ; and, at the same time,
cultivate the taste and judgment that are so indispensable for
understanding and enjoying works of art. A deeper feeling of
the beauties of music, and a more intellectual penetration of
its value, will result from the study of the works of great
masters ; more serious compositions will thus gain an attraction and a charm, which they did not before possess. Thus
we place an elevating element of thought in the room of
a trivial and unmeaning amusement, with which so many
hitherto have alone been acquainted, and to which they have
almost exclusively devoted their time and attention. But
whatever be the result at that age, it is unquestionable that
all these purposes will be better and more effectually attained
by those who have been brought up from their infancy with
music, who have known it as the companion of their youth,
and to whom it has necessarily become a study, full of interest and attraction, as delightful and consoling as it will be
inexhaustible.

Before we approach the examination of the moral influence of music, we conclude by recapitulating the principal
heads in the preceding remarks :—

1st, The earliest period of life is the best for the cultivation of the musical faculties.   The musical organs are
then easily developed, and defects corrected.

2d, Instead of being prejudicial to health, singing has been
found a powerful means of strengthening the lungs, throat,
and chest.

3d, Singing is the foundation of all musical education ; it
ought to precede the learning of any instrument.

IX.

Moral Influence of Music.—Songs for Children, their Poetical and Moral Character.

THAT music has a great power over man, and is capable of producing deep emotions, we all know, and we all have, once in our life at least, experienced: how sublime are the effects of a simple tune played on an instrument, or the solemn peal of the organ! and can it be believed that the human voice, the most impressive of all musical sounds, when joined to words, which speak at once to our feelings and our reason, does not, when thus adorned and rendered more significant, exert a greater and more beneficial influence upon our whole being than any other excitement? and must not this influence be materially increased, if we are ourselves the performers?

It is useless, however, to adduce further proofs, when thousands are ready to bear testimony to ·the vivid, the sublime, the powerful sentiments which song has often awakened within them, and to the beneficial and enduring impressions it has left behind. If such effects are felt by persons unprepared, perhaps, to receive high impressions, or in whom the gentler sensibilities have been blunted by the common drudgeries and troubles of life, how powerfully must the practice of singing, carefully adapted to this end, act upon the hearts and minds of children, whom the ills of existence have never reached, and whose soul is so innocently and defencelessly open and sensitive to impressions imparted from without. It must, therefore, be of great importance to every friend of youth, and every promoter of the interests of society, to know exactly the poetical and moral character of the compositions in which the youth of a country, the future nation, is to be instructed, and in whose hearts the impressions received, at such a tender age, will undoubtedly never be effaced. In this point consists the touch-stone of this question; here lie its public usefulness and its importance.

Juvenile poetry is in form and thought, we mean in the choice of the subject, as well as in that of the words employed to express it, of a peculiar kind. As soon as words are to be introduced into the exercises, too great care cannot be bestowed on their selection. Songs intended for children, should, in every respect, be adapted to the narrow limits of their understanding. They should present nothing abstract or inanimate, but should be full of life and action. The words of children's songs should treat of such innocent subjects as are suited to their years and feelings, if we desire that their effect upon them should be permanent and salutary. From songs of this character alone, the individual may derive benefit during his whole life, and may find in them aids to his moral and religious advancement. The child should receive from them such lessons as will add to the worthiness of the adult—lessons on all the duties he will have to perform, whether as a man, as a citizen, or as a link of that mighty chain called society.

The world appears to a child in a light totally different from that in which a grown-up person beholds it; his vivid imagination invests every object with life : in the buildings which his little hands raise out of sand, his creative fancy discovers cities, villages, and flowery fields; cards are converted into a palace; a fragment of glass furnishes a sun; a soap bubble is to him a world. The man of riper years, on the contrary, sees all his illusions vanish one by one; and as his feelings become hardened in the school of suffering and adversity, he gradually retires from the sphere of active existence, into a more abstract world of thought and recollection. He lives in the past, whilst the child—a butterfly, courting every flower, sucks its honied juice, and inhales its perfumes—knows and enjoys the present alone. In the rules, by which our choice of songs destined for children should be made, we should be guided by the nature of the infant mind itself, and should remember that the science of the child extends not further than its hand, and that the horizon of its mind closes with that of its eye.

Though there is a general dearth of songs for children, the materials for such songs are by no means so limited as may be supposed. All nature, as it lives around us, and spreads its charms and wonders out before our eyes—nature, with its hills and dales, its brooks, trees, birds, butterflies, and flowers, affords a varied choice of subjects, fitted to attract and interest the young mind.

In thus calling the attention of the young to nature in all its marvellous manifestations, we cannot fail to impress them with due respect for every object of the animate as well as inanimate creation. This has been overlooked in schools. Much is done for the intellect, but little for the heart, the main-spring of human actions in the social intercourse of life. How often are we forced to witness, in grief and indignation, the cruel pleasure that children (often intelligent and clever children in all that concerns the usual branches of instruction,) take in persecuting, and uselessly tormenting, animals, even those upon whose daily labours their own master's and tormentor's livelihood depends! General school instruction, as it is, is inadequate to develope the higher, better feelings, in children; and in trying to make them more learned, has utterly failed to make them more humane. Societies have been formed in all parts of Great Britain for the protection of animals. Prizes have been awarded, punishments inflicted. If, on one side, this proves that something is wanted in the education of the people, on the other, we can see at a glance the insufficiency of such societies. Unless man has learnt to respect the inferior beings in the scale of creation, and is moved by higher considerations than those of reward or punishment, such societies are of no avail, and, however well intended, do not attain the object of their foundation.

The children of our schools will never forget the lessons they received in songs which charmed their years of infancy;

they ever will remember the songs on *The Lark*, *The Bird's Nest*, *The Butterfly*, &c., &c. In shewing to them, in a few touching lines, the wondrous instinct of the *Sparrow*, the *Ant*, the *Bee*, &c., we cultivate in them that feeling of respect for all nature's children, which will follow them through life, and which will be their guide of conduct in all circumstances, when seen or when in solitude. Or can a song which delighted us in our infancy, pass without leaving a trace behind? Children, after having learnt by heart, and sung and enjoyed the sweet little strains on the *Fly*, would they ever forget the lessons they contain?

> My merry little fly play here,
> And let me look at you;
> I will not touch you, tho' you're near,
> As naughty children do.

> I'll near you stand to see you play,
> But do not be afraid;
> I would not lift my little hand
> To hurt the thing **He** made.

The same thought, only more sententiously expressed, pervades the little tune on *The Worm*. We quote it entire, because it illustrates distinctly our views and principles:—

> Turn, turn thy hasty foot aside,
> Nor crush this helpless worm;
> The frame thy thoughtless looks deride,
> Required a God to form.

> Let it enjoy its little day,
> Its little bliss receive;
> Oh! do not lightly take away
> The life thou canst not give.

Besides songs of this description, of whose importance in schools no one can doubt, there are also songs, intended to promote social and domestic virtues,—*order, cleanliness, obedience, unity, humanity, temperance*, &c.; thus impressing, not the letter of the laws of charity on immature minds, but the spirit of them in the memory, and so identifying them with the very fibres of the heart.

In all this we do not prescribe only vague theories, the execution of which exists but in the brain of an enthusiast, or belongs to future ages, we have seen them practically applied to the fullest extent. Juvenile compositions of that poetical and moral character which we recommend, already live in the mouths of thousands of children, and are heard in many a school and many a humble dwelling.

We should never cease, were we to tell of all the effects which, to our knowledge, the songs of children produced: they act upon the little singers, and re-act upon their parents. We know many families in which the children unite in the evening and sing their little duets, and through them charm and captivate those who hitherto sought recreation elsewhere than at their own hearth, in the society of their wives and children.

Music gives, as may easily be seen from this, to the home of the poorer classes, an additional attraction, and is a powerful, and at the same time elevating and noble substitute for those grosser pleasures which lead so many families into ruin and destitution; and, if what has been stated before Parliament be true, that the dissipated habits of the humbler classes have, for the most part, their source in the utter want of any rational enjoyment, and especially in the total intellectual destitution of the female part of the population, it must become a matter of considerable importance to see an innocent and elevating recreation like vocal music, associated with sacred and moral poetry, become a part of the education of the people. We pity those who know music only as a luxury, and who look with a jealous eye upon this art when taught to children, who are not born in and for the drawing-room, and who, therefore, have no right to claim their share of drawing-room education. Music is no luxury, but something far higher: we do not recognize it as such even among the wealthiest.

The education of the people has become the motto of all parties: if not from sympathy, humanity, and justice, its necessity is felt as the only means of self-defence against the daily growing stream of intemperance, poverty, depravity, and crime.[1] At the moment when popular education begins to be the all-engrossing subject of the Legislature, the warning lest mere intellectual education should exclusively occupy public attention, will neither be out of place nor out of season. Through its influence upon the youth of all classes, music must again become a serious object to serious minds, to the educationalist and the promoter of the moral advancement of the people. Herder says: ' To fill the whole soul of a child, to impart to him songs which will leave an impression, salutary and eternal; thus to urge him on to great actions, to glory; to implant in his heart the love of virtue, and to afford him consolation in that adversity which it may be his lot to encounter,—how noble an endeavour, how great a work!'

These few words of a profound thinker, a pious, noble, and classical mind, shew the great importance of this question; and we may conclude by saying, that music must again become an agent in the moral training of the people. Associated with poetry, simple and true, as a source from which heart and memory will, throughout life, draw lessons of virtue and morality, it will again be called the friend of humanity, the sister of wisdom.

[1] We refer the reader, for further particulars on this important subject, to Appendix No. II.

X.

FROM the preceding, it can be easily seen what musical instruction is, and how its influence might be applied with advantage to the education of youth. The errors committed in female schools can, therefore, not be raised as accusations against this art. " If you pray, or if you sing," says St Paul, "pray and sing with spirit and understanding." There is neither in the contemptible finger-stretching education, in the generality of educational institutions of that kind. That those who have thus learned music, or have thus seen it taught, are no friends to it, is not surprising; we would a thousand times prefer to see our children totally ignorant of the art, than that they should know it in its degradation.

The natural question now will be, Where should singing be taught, and how can it be acquired, according to which system, that it may become the key to all musical knowledge; and, above all, that the moral advantages, so much spoken of in the former part of this work, may be attained? Where shall we seek for our model? Where are the schools in which music has been so carefully associated with real training and real education? In Britain, France, or Germany? or in other continental states? Britain's period of musical supremacy has gone by; and after having once been a country which might, in point of composition, have vied with any of the continental nations, it is now satisfied with re-echoing the productions of German and Italian masters. In schools generally, as a branch of elementary instruction, it is but in germ; and only a few years are past since the proposition of its admission into schools, was received, by the whole House of the British Parliament, with a shout of laughter. France has, during the last thirty years, acknowledged its necessity, adopted it, by principle ; but it has, in fact, scarcely ever reached the suburbs of its great capital.

In Germany vocal music is everywhere adopted ; but nowhere has it received more careful attention, in the education of the people, than in Prussia. It seems, therefore, quite natural that in Germany, in Prussia particularly, we should seek the model for our musical constitution. And yet it is not so. Knowledge is acquired there, but not rightly applied ; it receives no right direction, and therefore misses or destroys the very purpose for which it is intended. The theatre has too much influence ; the opera too large a share in the music of all classes of society, even in schools ; it is cultivated, promoted by all possible means ; but that which gives to music its true importance, its power and influence, poetry, the indispensable partner, another self of this beautiful art, is not watched, not carefully enough selected, and zealously sounded in its moral bearing.

We follow, therefore, the footsteps of the ancients, and say that our music must be simple and characteristic ; that the poetry must be the best, and the purest in principle, adapted in tone and form to the various ages to which we address ourselves ; all that is great and good, cheering and elevating, must there find its musical and poetical accents.

In *Infant-schools*, children should learn little melodies, in poetry and music, according to the compass of their infantine intelligence and voice. They should sing *by heart* only ; nothing prepares better, and developes more effectually, than such early training, the musical faculties, the ear and voice, the feeling of time and rhythm.

In schools of children, (from 7 to 12 years of age,) singing at sight must become as general as the reading of the mother-tongue. This is the true age for musical instruction ; and schools of this kind are the true sphere in which it should breathe, grow, and be cultivated with care and solicitude. Children of all grades of society, whether boys or girls, in public, private, or charity schools ; in hospitals, orphan or blind asylums ; all must participate in this useful and pleasurable exercise.

As we intend to give to youth, that age of song, that season of poetry, poetry and song, no child should be deprived of the simple elements which can unfold to him so many moral treasures, so many hours of happiness : what is useful to one, is useful to all ; and if any instruction is to be considered universal, it is vocal music : upon its accents, moral lessons, sweet cheering lessons, are carried home, are retained in memory through life, in good and evil days.

When once acquainted with the elementary part of musical reading, and as we advance in age, a higher sphere of poetry opens itself ; the style of music will grow with the child. There are numerous smaller compositions in two and three parts required, which, without being as yet of a lofty character, may be beautiful in an humble sphere. All the finest shorter pieces of English poetry, simple in expression, noble in thought, clothed in analogous, melodious, and harmonious forms, might here find a place. In High-schools, classical academies, and in institutions for female education, this branch of instruction will rapidly reach maturity. The change, the animation, the cheerfulness which well-directed vocal classes will give to the inmates of houses of education, will be incalculable. The day classes, filled up with scientific subjects, will be succeeded by those of music, in which *all* can simultaneously be occupied. In the evening, the pupils of such institutions may again unite, and have their musical practisings. On holidays, or evenings of rest, what can be a substitute for a little family concert, where every one can join in some appropriate composition, beautiful and elevating, in poetry and music ? A better taste for the art will ere long manifest itself, and instrumental music may then have attractions to many who now may be justified in detesting it. Those who begin this movement with solidity and earnestness, will not regret it ; they will soon, as in

Germany, be the great models, objects of imitation to many others.[1]

Every school festivity, every examination or distribution of prizes, must be a day solemnized with music appropriate to the occasion. All the scholars must then take their part; the whole multitude of the now mute assembly of young people must become tuned and harmonized; at one given signal they must break forth in hundreds of voices, and open in solemn strains the solemnity of the day. Where is the classical scholar whose heart would not leap, in hearing hundreds of young voices strike up Fleming's simple composition of Horace's sublime *Integer vitae scelerisque purus?* who would not listen with emotion, after a silence of 1800 years, to the few specimens of ancient music: Misomedes's[2] Νέμεσι πτερόεσσα, or Pindar's Χρυσέα φόρμινξ᾽ Ἀπόλλωνος? How splendidly might, after a few voices had sung the first lines, the chorus Πείθονται δ᾽ ἀοιδοὶ σάμασιν appear, in full harmony, and sung by all the students of a High-school or a university!

If, after such modifications as time and circumstances have brought about in our day, ancient poetry and literature are still worthy of attention, those moments in which the best of the ancient poetical productions could be revived, and could again appear among us in the musical garments of which time has deprived them, would be of a high interest; they would make us more intimate with, and teach us more to enjoy, the inheritance left us by antiquity. Once more the voice of Horace and Ovid, Pindar, Alcæus, and Sappho, would be heard; and what, in the most inspired moments, their muse produced of the sublime and the beautiful, would resound again in our halls, would live on the tongue of a young

---

[1] " They began to employ vocal music as a means of education and mental refinement in the *Philanthropin* in Dessau; in the *elementary school* in Rekan, and in the *seminary* in Hanover. Encouraged by the most surprising results, one school and institution after another, imitated those models which had given the signal."—*Encyclopaedie der Tonkunst*, vol. v. article Music, p. 74.

[2] Misomedes of Crete, whom Eusebius calls in his *Chronicle*, κιθαρω-δικῶν νόμων μουσικὸς ποιητής.

generation, would again elevate, charm, and delight us. Instead of being shut up in our dusty libraries, songs will bring them nearer to our memory; the dead languages, the forgotten poets, those luminaries of the Grecian sky, will thus again rise out of their tomb: Greek will teach us music; music will teach us Greek; and the one will help us to raise the other in value and usefulness.

All these classes, at last, will reach that beautiful style, which, though scarcely known as yet, is that which gives to music its real character, its educational importance, the stamp of its lofty destiny,—*Domestic*, or *Family Music.* In a country where dramatic works have so long and so exclusively occupied the field, it is difficult to make it understood what family, what domestic music is. In the expectation that this style of composition would soon find poets and musicians, we might mention as such, the smaller pieces of Händel and Mozart, the psalms of Marcello; or, should we name the work of a more modern master, those beautiful duets of Rinck, called, in the English translation, " The Sabbath Eve !" In the character of these simple musical dialogues,[1] of which the English poet has unfortunately too much contracted the thought, is our idea of one kind of family music best personified. They have that sublime cast, that lofty tone and sentiment, which mark this kind of music as the most cheering, the most elevating. Who once has been a witness of the magic charm thrown over a family, by the true and expressive interpretation of such simple compositions; who has seen what a little paradise rises, as by enchantment, out of the few inspired strains of the poet-musician, will ever forget, what an endless ocean rolls its waves between the every-day compositions, and works, such as we understand them, and as we would fain see them domesticated under every roof, at every fireside ! The music we seek to implant in the soil and in the hearts of the people, is a music, the fruits of which render us wiser, better, and happier.[2] Why

[1] Published by Ewer & Co., Newgate Street.

[2] Thibaut, the celebrated Professor of Law in Heidelberg, in whose house the best compositions of the 16th and 17th centuries were perform-

should not, in every family, when the day's busy stream is past, all unite harmoniously, and have one happy hour in the enjoyment of such works?

To attain all this, the means are simple: Vocal music must be acknowleged as an indispensable branch of instruction in every school. The young scholar must be made aware that he is learning something useful; as a renovating and exhilarating power, the music-lesson must be placed between those studies which require more mental abstraction. There is no hope of seeing music and poetry resume their power in education, until teachers begin to understand that an hour devoted to their acquirement, is not an hour lost, but an hour gained for school and church, for life and for society.

Another question now presents itself, that of the most suitable method of imparting to the young the necessary musical elements. Nothing is more important, and it cannot be denied, that one method is preferable to the other, as being based upon simpler principles, and more in conformity with the juvenile capacities and juvenile understanding. But should it be made obligatory on the teacher? Supposing the system he wishes to follow simple and easy, based upon the nature of the art to be learnt, and the intelligence and the nature of the child who has to acquire it, and therefore perfectly well adapted for schools,—is he to be prevented from carrying it out? Should, because one method has become the law of the land, the world of thought and of inquiry be shut up to all future improvement and progress? should all studies, all efforts, be thus declared useless and unavailable? No country has ever attempted such tyranny. Neither France nor Prussia, neither Saxony, Bavaria, nor Würtenberg, have ever dared to put such drag-shoes on human intelligence, the least of all on educational pursuits. School books are examined with care, and, above all, by men competent to judge; and when approved, they are re-

ed, relates, in his musical work, *Ueber Reinheit der Tonkunst*, of a young man, who, after hearing a composition of Lotti, was so moved, that in leaving his house, he exclaimed, " Oh! this evening, I could do no harm to my greatest enemy."

commended, but their exclusive use is never insisted upon.
Numerous methods bear, therefore, in France the words,
Approuvée et recommandée, as motto of the minister of public
instruction : so it is in Germany : hundreds of different methods are thus, at the same time, in operation : here it is
the one, there the other, which produces the better result,
according to circumstances or the individuality of the teacher.
Make the teacher answerable for the result, but leave to him
the choice of the means.   He knows best how to work, in
order to reach the mind of infancy.   His system may not be
the best, yet he will imbue it with an element without which
the most perfect method remains a dead letter, a closed, an
unintelligible book,—the fire of his heart, his enthusiasm.

The Board of Education in England has, during the last
few years, given a half-official acknowledgment to music.   It
is a timid commencement of a great period in the history of
music in Great Britain ; this period has, however, not begun
under favourable circumstances.   What is given with the
one hand, is destroyed with the other.   And, contradictory
as it seems to the national feeling and the national habits,
Great Britain is the country in which this branch of education has been made a monopoly.   All other methods or
systems of teaching, are under the ban of the Board of Education : far from deserving encouragement, they are treated
as tares, good only to be uprooted and perish on the high-
way.   Musical methods have breathed their last ; the philosophical stone has been discovered ! and teachers and theo-
rists, for all time to come, may rest in peace, and stretch their
limbs under the shade of this Herculean pillar of the human
intellect.[1] If you really wish that music should lay hold of the

---

[1] This plan, so passionately pursued by the Secretary of the Board of
Education, has found in the public press a still more violent advocate.
The Athenæum, which pretends to the honour of leading the destiny
of art in Great Britain, has, in its "Weekly Gossip," become the trumpeter
of the new musical Joshua.   Whether the musical world, especially
those numerous teachers who have in this field for years exerted themselves successfully, will acknowledge such doubtful superiority, and
doubtful disinterestedness, we cannot say ; we know only, that every one
who has studied music seriously, must be convinced that something more

young population, and penetrate into the very heart of the British islands, throw widely open the gates of instruction ; surround yourself with a whole army of different teachers and different systems ! efface the line of narrow demarcation, and let the stream of competition carry on its waves, life and animation, through the schools, into the people. Give some special encouragement to this so neglected art, and some preference to the schoolmaster able to promote it. Try enlarged ideas, and see whether they are not more worthy of a great nation. All the youth of your country will then be instructed, never mind by what plan or system. Let Progress be your standard, and do not force us, since we have steamers and railroads, to travel in sedans and litters, on horses and donkies, as our forefathers did.

In this manner you will soon see, one after another, the schools begin the work ; the success of one will be a stimulus to all ; and, by degrees, there will be no re-union of young persons or young students, of children or infants, no orphans, and no inmates of a charity school, from the Channel to the islands of Ultima Thule, where the hundreds and the thousands will not raise their voices, and surprise and overpower every ear and every heart.

Thus, when a competition is opened for methods and systems, as well as for poetical and musical compositions, lofty in thought and beautiful in form, and, in every respect, fit to take a share in the education of the people ; a new and important branch of composition will appear as by enchantment, and extend its influence and ramifications into every school and every family through the length and breadth of the land. The educational and family music, scarcely known as yet by name, will, in the midst of an ocean, in all its various changes and tempests, stand in its simplicity, purity,

is to be done for its advancement than gossiping about it ; that there is a great distance from understanding music to talking musical trivialities; and that he who is guilty of the " Weekly Gossip," and therefore proves that he stands but in the antechamber of art, should certainly not presume to judge, when so important a matter as musical education is the subject.

and grandeur. like a rock, and bear unshaken the sway of all the surrounding tides of style and fashion. May the classic, romantic, and fantastic schools, combat and efface each other! may the lyric drama of all the continental languages intoxicate the lions of the fashionable world! there will be a music which appears neither upon the stage nor the market-place, neither in concerts nor drawing-rooms, but which modestly enlivens the school and the cottage, and helps to instruct the people, to embellish the hour of toil and that of rest. This style will remain uncontaminated by the impure breath of changing fashion and passing mountebanks, and as truly NATIONAL, form the axis, round which all others move, appear and disappear, as figures of a *Lanterna Magica*. In this manner you will render to the young what they have been deprived of; you will advance the rest of Europe, and give, even to Prussia, a glorious example of a better, a more philosophical application of music to the education of youth.

Thus Music will again be looked at with reverence. In churches she will fill, like a stream, the hearts of the multitude ; she will again appear as the minstrel and the harp of old in our dwelling ; be our guardian angel, a heavenly messenger, our teacher, friend, and comforter ; and from her deepest dejection, from a state of servitude, corruption, and degeneracy, rise, a new phœnix out of ashes, higher and higher, to a glorious apotheosis.

APPENDIX I.

AN opinion contrary to that of Aristotle was very often entertained in ancient and modern times. Philip of Macedon reproached his son Alexander with himself practising music, instead of being content to listen to that of others. The same opinion was expressed, in our times, by a man whose influence was considerable on the fashionable world, and whose reasonings still influence those who have been educated, or continue to educate, upon such superficial and formal principles. It was about the middle of last century that music was probably at its lowest ebb in England, and the contemptuous language used by Lord Chesterfield, in regard to its practice, may be taken as an indication of the way of thinking on that subject among the fashionable society of his day. He says, "If you love music, hear it : pay fiddlers to play to you, but never fiddle yourself. It makes a gentleman appear frivolous and contemptible; leads him frequently into bad company, and wastes that time which otherwise might be well employed." Lord Chesterfield's condensed and sententious style, gives his precepts a false air of soundness and truth ; they have led many a weak head into the conviction, that he could not be a perfect gentleman without following the instructions, and emulating the example, of so great a master. There are thousands who mistake the outside, with all its hollowness and glitter, for the internal and essential truth, and adopt Lord Chesterfield's precepts as their manual, both in their moral and intellectual education. A mind so constituted can know little or nothing of moral and spiritual worth. Outward forms, and a little brilliant appearance in society, are the main points to which Lord Chesterfield's maxims are directed. What marvel, then, that art in general, and more particularly music, is never understood by men of this stamp, whose whole scope

G

is not to be, but to appear perfect. His words, when more closely examined, are the expression either of consummate ignorance, or an overweening idea of what is due to dignity and decorum. That music is not for a gentleman, says as little as the known words of Charles II., that the Presbyterian religion was not a religion for a gentleman.

The opinion of Lord Chesterfield might be easily balanced with that of other men, whose names stand in history so high, that neither the frivolous nor the contemptible of his Lordship's musical anathema can reach them.

Charlemagne not only, according to Eginhard, ordered all national songs to be collected, not only instituted music schools, but sang himself with the choir in church. Almost the whole series of the Austrian emperors were practical musicians ; some, even eminent composers.

Leopold I. was not only an excellent pianist, but his airs and cantatas, many of which are still extant, are proofs of his talent and skill. It is said, in the life of Leopold the Great, (published at Leipzig, 1709,) that the Emperor preferred music to every other enjoyment. In each of his four palaces, in which he used to pass alternately a certain time, there was a valuable harpsichord in his private apartment, and at this instrument he passed all his leisure hours. All the members of his chapel, musicians, leaders, and singers, were examined by himself before their reception ; and it was merit only, not favour, which influenced his choice. His chapel was therefore esteemed the first in Europe. Many of the members were counts and barons, and their appointments were such as enabled them to live in a manner becoming their families. Not an opera was represented, for which the Emperor had not composed one or more airs. During the performance, he had the score constantly before him, and followed the performers with the utmost attention. When a passage made a particular impression on him, he closed his eyes, but opened them very wide when anybody in the orchestra committed a mistake ; on these occasions he generally pointed out the offender.

Joseph I. inherited his predecessor's love for music. Charles VI. also held it in high estimation, promoted its culture, and was himself a performer on several instruments. During his reign, music was much cultivated by persons of the first families. His inclinations led him especially to dramatic music. The poet of his court, Metastasio, contributed not a little to this predilection. Caldara's splendid work, *Achilles*, was performed at the nuptials of Maria Therese.

Fuchs, the great composer, and author of the celebrated *Gradus ad Parnassum,* was the aulic Kapellmeister during the reign of these three emperors. In the year 1724, on the birthday of one of the Austrian archduchesses, one of Fuchs's operas was performed, which pleased the Emperor to such a degree, that he set on foot a lottery for all who performed in it, in which every one had to gain from 500 to 2000 florins. The Emperor himself played, and conducted the performance at the harpsichord. It was at this representation that Kapellmeister Fuchs (who stood behind the Emperor, and turned the leaves of the score,) was so much enchanted, in a passage of great difficulty, with the Emperor's skill, that he loudly exclaimed, " Bravo !" and added, " Your Majesty might be employed as a most accomplished Kapellmeister." The Emperor turned his head, and said, " I am pretty well satisfied with my situation."

Joseph II. was also a musician, and sang very well. The operas of Gluck, Paesiello, Cimarosa, Martini, Salieri, and Sarti, were performed at the theatre of the Court before the public in Vienna.

Frederick the Great was a passionate lover of music; and though a first-rate flute player, was not less a first-rate soldier, the terror of the Russian and Austrian armies. After he had been rushing against the enemies' batteries, and had roared like a lion to his dispersing squadrons his favourite cry, " *Will you, then, live for ever !*" he was an hour later heard, in his tent, playing on the flute.—Alexander I., Emperor of Russia, to whom music had been, as to Frederick the Great, in the strongest terms forbidden by his father, loved and practised it all his life.—We know from what has been stated, (p. 57 and 58,) that in the most brilliant period of the English annals, the reign of Queen Elizabeth, musical skill and knowledge were so essential to persons of condition, that ignorance of the art was looked upon as a proof of low breeding, and unfitness for the intercourse of polite society. A thousand examples of this kind might be gathered from the history of all nations. A number of the English kings were musicians : the Stuarts of Scotland were remarkably skilled in this art. James I. was one of the first musicians of his age, and most accomplished on every instrument.

If Lord Chesterfield is an authority, Milton is another, perhaps a greater one ; and it is when speaking precisely of the education of young gentlemen, that he says, "The rest before meat may, both with profit and delight, be taken up in recreating and composing their travail'd spirits, with the solemn and divine harmonies of music *heard* or *learn'd;* either while the skilful organist plies his grave and fancied descant in lofty fugues, or the whole symphony, with artful and imaginable touches, adorn and grace the well-studied chords of some choice composer ; sometimes the lute or soft organ stop waiting on elegant voices, either to religious, martial, or civil ditties, which, if wise men and prophets be not extremely out, have a great power over dispositions and manners, to smoothe and make them gentle from rustic harshness and distemper'd passions." [1]

J. J. Rousseau was not only a musical copyist, he was also a theorist and composer. His opera, *Le Divin du Village,* has seen more representations than any opera ever since performed. Upon the volume of songs composed by him, he wrote the remarkable words : "La consolation des misères de ma vie."

To conclude, we might reply to Lord Chesterfield, what Count d'Anjou answered to his cousin Louis d'Outremer, who reproached him with practising music himself, instead of doing it by deputy : "Sachez, Sire, qu'un Roi sans musique, n'est qu'un âne couronné."

[1] Milton's *Letter on Education.*

APPENDIX II.

POLYBIUS says (Hist. iv., 20) : " With regard to the inhabitants of Cynætha, whose misfortunes we have just now mentioned, it is certain that no people ever were esteemed so justly to deserve that cruel treatment to which they were exposed. And since the Arcadians, in general, have been always celebrated for their virtue throughout all Greece, and have obtained the highest fame, as well by their humane and hospitable disposition, as from their piety also towards the gods, and the veneration of all things sacred; it may perhaps be useful to enquire from whence it could arise, that the people of this single city, though confessed to be Arcadians, should, on the contrary, be noted for the savage roughness of their lives and manners, and distinguished by their wickedness and cruelty above all the Greeks. In my judgment, then, this difference has happened from no other cause than that the Cynætheans were the first and only people among the Arcadians who threw away that institution which their ancestors had established with the greatest wisdom, and with a nice regard to the natural genius and peculiar disposition of the people of the country ; I mean, the discipline and exercise of music ; of that genuine and perfect music, which is useful indeed in every state, but absolutely necessary to the people of Arcadia. For we ought by no means to adopt the sentiment that is thrown out by Ephorus in the preface to his history, and which indeed is very unworthy of that writer, ' That music was invented to deceive and delude mankind.' Nor can it be supposed, that the Lacedæmonians and the ancient Cretans were not influenced by some great reason, when, in the place of trumpets, they introduced the sound of flutes, and harmony of verse, to animate their soldiers in the time of battle; or that the first Arcadians acted without strong necessity, who, though their lives and manners, in all other points, were rigid and austere, incorporated this art into the very essence of their government ; and obliged not their children only, but the young men likewise, till they had gained the age of thirty years, to persist in the constant study and practice of it. For all men know that Arcadia is almost the only country in which the children, even from their most tender age, are taught to sing, in measure, their songs and hymns that are composed in honour of their gods and heroes : and that afterwards, when they have learned the music of Timotheus and Philoxenus, they assemble once in every year in the public theatres, at the feast of Bacchus, and there dance, with emulation, to the sound of flutes, and celebrate, according to their proper age, the children, those that are called the puerile, and the young men, the manly games ; and even in their private feasts and meetings, they are never known to employ any hired bands of music for their entertainment, but each man is obliged himself to sing in turn. For though they may, without shame or censure, disown all knowledge of every other science, they dare not, on the one hand, dissemble or deny that they are skilled in music, since the laws require that every one should be instructed in it; nor can they, on the other hand, refuse to give some proofs of their skill when asked, because such refusal would be esteemed dishonourable. They are also taught to perform, in order, all the military steps and motions to the sound of instruments : and this is likewise practised every year in the theatres, at the public charge, and in sight of all the citizens.

" Now, to me it is clearly evident, that the ancients by no means introduced these customs to be the instruments of luxury and idle pleasure ; but because they had considered with attention, both the painful and laborious course of life to which the Arcadians were accustomed, and the natural austerity also of their manners, derived to them from that cold and heavy air, which covered the greatest part of all their province. For men will be always found to be in some degree assimilated to the climate in which they live : nor can it be ascribed to any other cause, that in the several nations of the world, distinct and separated from each other, we behold so wide a difference in complexion, features, manners, and customs. The Arcadians, therefore, in order to smoothe and soften that disposition which was by nature so rough and stubborn, besides the customs above described, appointed frequent festivals and sacrifices, which both sexes were required to celebrate together ; the men with women, and the boys with virgins; and, in general, established every institution that could serve to render their rugged minds more gentle and compliant, and tame the fierceness of their manners. But the people of Cynætha, having slighted all these arts, though both their air and situation, the most inclement and unfavourable of any in Arcadia, made some such remedy more requisite to them than to the rest, were afterwards engaged continually in intestine tumults and contentions, till they became at last so fierce and savage, that, among all the cities of Greece, there was none in which so many and so great enormities were ever known to be committed. To how deplorable a state this conduct had at last reduced them, and how much their manners were detested by the Arcadians, may be fully understood from that which happened to them, when they sent an embassy to Lacedæmon, after the time of a dreadful slaughter which had been made among them. For in every city of Arcadia through which their deputies were obliged to pass, they were commanded by the public crier instantly to be gone. The Mantineans also expressed even still more strongly their abhorrence of them; for, as soon as they were departed, they made a solemn purification of the place, and carried their victims in procession round the city, and through all their territory.

"This, then, may be sufficient to exempt the general customs of Arcadia from all censure; and, at the same time, to remind the people of that province, that music was at first established in their government, not for the sake of mere pleasure and amusement, but for such solid purposes as should engage them never to desert the practice of it. The Cynætheans also may perhaps draw some advantage from these reflections, and, if the Deity should hereafter bless them with better sentiments, may turn their minds towards such discipline, as may soften and improve their manners, and especially to music, by which means alone they can ever hope to be divested of that brutal fierceness for which they have been so long distinguished."

If Polybius were still among us, and visited our poor-houses, lunatic asylums, and prisons, he would still say, that criminals and insane are so, out of all proportion, numerous, because the first and simplest of all means of education, music, has been neglected. However ludicrous this may appear to some of our legislators and educationalists, yet nothing would be more true. If the people of Great Britain had learned music as an amusement only, they would not want to seek amusement in public houses; and there is the source of their ruin, ruin in health and in character. The state seems to find prisons and lunatic asylums indispensable institutions, or it would stop the source whence the insane and criminals proceed. Shut up public houses, teach the people sober habits for those of intemperance, and soon you will have to close the greater number of the asylums and the jails. Would it not be better to inspire the people with purer desires, and to provide them with nobler amusements? Teach them in your schools those innocent pleasures which music gives, and you will make their home more attractive. Where is the husband debased enough, who would seek pleasures abroad, when the mother sits by the fireside, surrounded by her children, and sings sacred hymns or songs, appropriate in music and poetry, to time and circumstances! Or is, then, in reality the vice of intemperance so ineffaceable in the British Islands? have not philanthropists gathered the most terrifying statistics of the increase of this fearful epidemic, which undermines the physical and moral health of families, of cities, and of the state, and augments daily, to a degree quite alarming, the destitute and the criminal? And are we not the authors, should they one day, in overwhelming multitudes, range themselves in armies, and under the command of a bold tribune, seek to revenge themselves for their depraved habits and their crimes in which the state has nourished them, for their bodily and mental destitution in which the state has left them, and from which it made not even an attempt to redeem them, although forewarned in a thousand ways?

Well may be heard here the voice of a French writer who has studied the dangerous classes of society, and has written on them a remarkable work. Although under different circumstances, in a different age, his words say nothing that is not expressed in those of Polybius; yet as they speak of the dangerous classes of that society with which we have to come in daily contact, which live with us in the same city, in the same street, and under the same roof, his remarks will come closer home, and find, at least, a more interested reception.

" The singing classes have a relation to the amusements of the people ; and for this reason it is, perhaps, that they have been judged less favourably than those courses of instruction which had reference to objects purely utilitarian. It has been said that they are not in harmony with the condition of those for whom they are designed. The objection is not a conclusive one ; for the most brilliant airs of our operas are daily hawked about our streets, and sung in our highways. These airs, caught flying, if we may so express ourselves, by the workmen, are repeated in their shops and garrets. Why forbid them access to the punctuated music and accentuated harmonies of scientific compositions, when you cannot prevent their seizing, and rendering often with great taste, by their musical instinct alone, the airs which float through the works of our greatest masters. The municipal administration may not as yet have fully satisfied itself as to the utility of the moral and civil effects which will result from the funds granted for the establishment of these music classes; for unhappily there is, even among the enlightened, a disposition to believe that the people are not susceptible of the charm of noble or refined amusements, or of emotions which are purely intellectual. Yet it is a fact in evidence, that such amusements have an irresistible attraction for them. I am anxious to point out this error, and call attention to the facts which attest it, because it is most mischievous.

" In truth, our rulers and political economists, have reflected too little on the moral bearing of public amusements—on those especially adapted to the labouring classes. Yet amusement of some kind is a necessity of all ages and all conditions. The poorer a man is, and the more he is the slave of toil, the more needful it is that he should find diversion and refreshment of some kind for his weary spirit; and the more important that he should find it in enjoyments which are not sensual, and which, while they soothe his feelings, refine them. The human heart is naturally so unquiet, morose, and jealous a thing, so apt to make *itself* the *centre* of all its thoughts and sentiments, that the happiest man is he who can most easily find the means of escaping from his own narrow personality, to fix his attention on something which is not himself.

" Interest him in the recital of some noble action, excite him by verses or songs which give expression to lofty sentiments, or paint the beautiful features of natural scenery, and you will see him rejoice in his own emotions, mastered and melted by the omnipotence of the arts.

" Music, the most seductive and the purest of them all, is calculated, more than all, to exercise a sway over the popular heart, raising therein sensations alternately glowing and refined."[1]

In a work of the same kind—*The Claims of Labour*,—the same idea is expressed thus :—

[1] H. Regier, *Des Classes dangereuses de la Société.*

" We may remark, as bearing upon this subject, that singing lessons should be greatly encouraged in schools. There are several merits connected with this mode of instruction. It employs many together, and gives a feeling of communion ; it is not much mixed up with emulation ; the tenderest and highest sentiments may be unostentatiously impressed by its means, for you can introduce in songs such things as you could not lecture upon ; then it gives somewhat of a cultivated taste, and an additional topic of social interest, even to those who do not make much proficiency ; while to others, who have a natural ability for it, it may form an innocent and engaging pursuit throughout their lives."

The voice for an improved state of the education of the people has been raised repeatedly and eloquently by Lord Ashley, Mr Wyse, and many others. Mr Wyse, who was almost the first who brought the question of music, in its connection with a national system of education, before the British public and the British Parliament,[1] says :—Music, even the most elementary, not only does not form an essential of education in this country, but the idea of introducing it is not even dreamt of. It is urged, that it would be fruitless to attempt it, because the people are essentially anti-musical ; but may not they be anti-musical, because it has not been attempted ? The people roar and scream, because they have heard nothing but roaring and screaming—no music—from their childhood. Is harmony not to be taught ? is it not to be extended ? is not a taste to be generated, at least in the period of two generations ? Taste is the habit of good things ; " je ne suis pas la rose, mais j'ai vecu avec elle," is to be caught. But the inoculation must somewhere or other begin. It is this apathy about beginning that is censurable, not the difficulty of propagating when it has once appeared. No effort is made in any of our schools ; and then we complain that there is no music amongst scholars. It would be just as reasonable to exclude grammar, and then complain that we had no grammarians. . . . . *The elements of music should, therefore, form an integral part of all public education.* . . . . A better preservative of pure morals ; a more delightful addition to innocent amusements ; a more cheerful stimulant to all exercises, whether of labour, study, or religion, can scarcely be devised. Nor would its effects be confined to the school-room or to childhood ; it would soon penetrate the paternal dwelling ; in another generation it would be natural to the land."

---

[1] *Education Reform*, by T. Wyse, Esq., M.P , pp. 186 and 195.

Mr W. E. Hickson, who has done so much for education, and has devoted himself so earnestly to the promotion of music in schools, has, like a true statesman, penetrated this subject.[1] He shews how miserably deficient are our present systems of education ; how they work only upon the intellect, and upon that imperfectly, and neglect the cultivation of the heart ; how our poorer classes, especially, are taught only a few barren mechanical acquirements, such as reading, writing, and casting accounts, whilst their honest sympathies, their generous emotions, their whole moral natures, are altogether uncared for and unattended to. After urging that education should embrace a higher, nobler object than these mechanical acquirements ; that every moral engine by which the character can be influenced and improved, should be employed ; and after briefly explaining how music exerts its power, he proceeds to shew that vocal music, judiciously directed, is a most efficient means of moralization.

"Music may be regarded as having an indirect moral influence in weaning the mind from coarse and brutalizing pursuits, and from pleasures consisting in mere sensual indulgences. The reason is, that music is a means of pure and innocent enjoyment, which, in proportion as it is cultivated and directed, will approve itself to the mind, as of a higher, better, and more satisfactory character, than any of the grosser pleasures pursued by the slaves of vice.

" And here let me protest against the doctrine, that it is not part, or ought to be no part, of the business of an instructor, to teach the means of rational enjoyment to the people. That music is a means of social enjoyment, will be admitted ; and that ought to be a sufficient argument for rendering it, if possible, a means of enjoyment to the poorest of the community. After all that can be done for the amelioration of the condition of the working-classes, they will have to submit to quite enough of privation, as compared with the lot of a rich man, without withholding from them any innocent source of pleasure which we might enable them to command.

" I have no sympathy with those who think that the duty of individuals or of legislators, with regard to the masses, ends in teaching them resignation and submission, and in enabling them at best to earn their bread by the sweat of their brow; but who

---

[1] A *Lecture*, by W. E. Hickson, on the introduction of VOCAL MUSIC as a branch of national education. Taylor and Walton.

would do nothing to cheer their hearts or gladden their existence, by throwing a little sunshine into the cottage, as if nature had designed them to be merely living, moving, animated machines, existing not for themselves, but solely to furnish the means of gratification to a superior race of mortals.

" Happily, however, for the lot of the poor, nature has not left it to our own cold hearts to decide this question. Some amount of pleasurable relaxation from labour is necessary to every condition of animal existence. The slave will have it, though he work in chains for six days out of the seven, or without it he will die, and thus escape the lash of his cruel task-master. Some change of a pleasurable character, to relieve the monotony of a life of labour, is necessary for all; but, what is most to the purpose, we can withhold it from none—we can merely choose the form it shall assume.

" This is then the real question at issue, whether we shall leave the people, while in a low moral state, to choose their own sources of gratification, (although we may know that while in that state, they will choose such as will be of a low and debasing character,) or shall we first enable them to appreciate, and then place within their reach rational and intellectual enjoyments? In short, will you have prize-fighting, bull-baiting, gambling, Tom and Jerry amusements, a taste encouraged for witnessing executions and reading of murders ; will you have intemperance, as a means of excitement, rendered all but universal ; or will you allow an art like that of music to be cultivated in their place, and teach society to obey the laws of harmony, both in a moral and scientific sense ?"

In the same spirit are written the following eloquent lines by Dr Channing, in his *Address on Temperance :*—

" The first means which I shall suggest of placing a people beyond the temptation to intemperance, is to furnish them with the means of innocent pleasure.

" I have said, a people should be guarded against temptation to unlawful pleasures, by furnishing the means of innocent ones. By innocent pleasures, I mean such as excite moderately ; such as produce a cheerful frame of mind, not boisterous mirth ; such as refresh, instead of exhausting the system ; such as recur frequently, rather than continue long ; such as send us back to our daily duties invigorated in body and in spirit ; such as we can partake in the presence and society of respectable friends ; such as consist with, and are favourable to, a grateful piety ; such as are chastened by self-respect, and are accompanied with the consciousness that life has a higher end than to be amused. In every community there must be pleasures, relaxations, and means of agreeable excitement; and if innocent ones are not furnished, resort will be had to criminal. Man was made to enjoy, as well as to labour, and the state of society should be adapted to this principle of human nature. France, especially before the Revolution, has been represented as a singularly temperate country; a fact to be explained, at least in part, by the constitutional cheerfulness of that people, and the prevalence of simple and innocent gratifications, especially among the peasantry. Men drink to excess very often to shake off depression, or to satisfy the restless thirst for agreeable excitement, and these motives are excluded in a cheerful community. A gloomy state of society, in which there are few innocent recreations, may be expected to abound in drunkenness, if opportunities are afforded. The savage drinks to excess, because his hours of sobriety are dull and unvaried, because, in losing the consciousness of his condition and his existence, he loses little which he wishes to retain. The labouring classes are most exposed to intemperance, because they have at present few other pleasurable excitements. A man, who, after toil, has resources of blameless recreation, is less tempted than other men to seek self-oblivion. He has too many of the pleasures of a man, to take up with those of a brute. Thus, the encouragement of simple innocent enjoyments is an important means of temperance.

" These remarks shew the importance of encouraging the efforts which have commenced among us, for spreading the accomplishment of music through our whole community. It is now proposed that this shall be made a regular branch in our schools; and every friend of the people must wish success to the experiment. I am not now called to speak of all the good influences of music, particularly of the strength which it may and ought to give to the religious sentiment, and to all pure and generous emotions. Regarded merely as a refined pleasure, it has a favourable bearing on public morals. Let taste and skill in this beautiful art be spread among us, and every family will have a new resource. Home will gain a new attraction. Social intercourse will be more cheerful; and an innocent public amusement will be furnished to the community. Public amusements bringing multitudes together, to kindle with one emotion, to share the same innocent joy, have an humanizing influence; and among these bonds of society, perhaps no one produces so much unmixed good as music. What a fulness of enjoyment has our Creator placed within our reach, by surrounding us with an atmosphere which may be shaped into sweet sounds? And yet this goodness is almost lost upon us, through want of culture of the organ by which this provision is to be enjoyed."

Madame de Stael[1] says :—

" There is a whole order of sentiments, I might say, a whole order of virtues, which belong to the knowledge, or at least to the taste for music ; and it is great barbarity to deprive a numerous portion of the human race of such impressions. The ancients pretended that nations had been civilized by music, and this allegory has a deep meaning ; for we must always suppose that the bond of society was formed either by sympathy or interest, and certainly the first origin is more noble than the other."

Napoleon, the mortal enemy of Madame de Stael, had not less than herself a very peculiar predilection for music; and remarkable is his opinion on this art, expressed in these words :—" Music exercises the greatest influence upon the human passions, and acts with an uncommon power upon man. It is a duty of the legislator to encourage and to favour the study of music more than any other art. A moral composition, drawn by the hand of a master, penetrates into the deepest feelings, and operates more powerfully than any good and moral work which speaks to our reason only."

In the *Manuel de l'Instruction Primaire*, (c. vii. art. 1,) addressed to the teachers throughout France, we read, " Le chant élève l'ame et touche le cœur : il est une partie intégrante du culte, et un divertissement pour le peuple. *Il sera donc un moyen puissant d'éducation dans toutes les écoles primaires.*"

After having given more detailed regulations on the singing exercises to be applied to children, the minister of public instruction continues in the same *Manuel*, (c. vii. art. 4,) in which vocal music is considered as an essential, and not an accessory branch of popular education : "On parviendra de cette manière à faire chanter convenablement dans l'église, *à ennoblir les idées, à toucher les cœurs, à évincer les mauvaises chansons populaires, à réformer la morale publique.*"

The minister of war in France has, a short time ago, published an ordinance, in which the organization of vocal choirs is commanded in every regiment. In Germany, such bands consist often of the whole regiment. We hope to see the British army imitate such examples. Nothing is easier than to reach with whole battalions

---

[1] De Stael on *Germany*, Volume I. chap. 19th : (*On Public Institutions.*)

this result. A few of the many hours which burden the existence of the soldier, and which are so often spent in worse than idleness, might be spared during the week for musical instruction. Every regiment would soon have its vocal band, and soon we would reach those great results described by Ambert :[1]—

"La grande voix du régiment se ferait entendre ; les compagnies répondraient aux compagnies, et les bataillons marcheraient avec l'orgueil des cohortes anciennes.—Oh! alors je n'en doute pas, les choses miraculeuses que le fanatisme faisait exécuter jadis se renouvelleraient de nos jours."

We cannot refrain from quoting, in regard to the musical instruction in regiments, the eloquent lines of Guéroult :—

"Pour donner une grande impulsion, je ne sache rien de plus efficace que l'éducation musicale de l'armée ; il faut que l'art sorte aujourd'hui de ces petits tabernacles bourgeois ; il faut qu'il descende dans le peuple, et qu'il aille chercher des recrues dans ses derniers rangs. Or, l'armée c'est le peuple assemblé, le peuple discipliné, hiérarchisé, organisé ; c'est une députation du peuple prête à recevoir le feu sacré pour le porter ensuite sur toute la surface du territoire. Le peuple est aujourd'hui la grande pépinière où les partis épuisés vont se renouveler ; rien de grand ne se fait aujourd'hui qu'en son nom, qu'au nom de ses intérêts.—Que le savoir donc soit distribué au peuple, que l'industrie s'occupe de son bien-être, il y a là pour des siècles de travaux ; mais que l'art aussi ait sa part dans les libéralités de ses puissans amis. Nous le demandons pour le peuple et pour l'art : pour le peuple, que l'art annoblira, élèvera, moralisera ; pour l'art, qui, armé de la voix puissante du peuple, pourra enfin sortir des serres-chaudes où il est cultivé, et pousser ses racines en pleine terre, en plein vent, en pleine humanité. Je le dis avec une entière conviction, le jour où l'art quittera les boudoirs pour la place publique, une révolution plus grande aura été accomplie que lorsque de l'église il est monté sur le théâtre. Oui, faisons de la démocratie en musique ; ce sera une démocratie bienfaisante, pacifique ; toute à l'avantage de tous."

[1] *Esquisses historiques des Armées Françaises,* par Joachim Ambert.

F I N I S.

PRINTED BY H. AND J. PILLANS, EDINBURGH.

For EU product safety concerns, contact us at Calle de José Abascal, 56–1°,
28003 Madrid, Spain or eugpsr@cambridge.org.

www.ingramcontent.com/pod-product-compliance
Ingram Content Group UK Ltd.
Pitfield, Milton Keynes, MK11 3LW, UK
UKHW040616240426
470322UK00010B/150